THE
EASTERN
AIRLINES
STRIKE

THE EASTERN AIRLINES STRIKE

Accomplishments of the Rank-and-File Machinists and Gains for the Labor Movement

by Ernie Mailhot, Judy Stranahan, and Jack Barnes

PATHFINDER

New York   London   Montréal   Sydney

Edited by John Riddell

ISBN 0-87348-626-9 paper; ISBN 0-87348-635-8 cloth
Library of Congress Catalog Card Number 91-60839
Manufactured in the United States of America

First edition, 1991

Cover and book design by Toni Gorton and Eric Simpson

Front cover photo: Picket line outside Eastern Shuttle terminal at
New York's La Guardia Airport, March 6, 1989. (Ernie Mailhot/*Militant*) Back cover photo: Eastern strike contingent at Philadelphia
Labor Day parade, September 4, 1989. (Kathy Mickells/*Militant*)

Pathfinder
410 West Street, New York, NY 10014, U.S.A.

Pathfinder distributors around the world:
Australia (and Asia and the Pacific):
  Pathfinder, 19 Terry St., Surry Hills, Sydney, NSW 2010
Britain (and Europe, Africa, and the Middle East):
  Pathfinder, 47 The Cut, London, SE1 8LL
Canada:
  Pathfinder, 6566, boul. St-Laurent, Montréal, Québec, H2S 3C6
Iceland:
  Pathfinder, Klapparstíg 26, 2d floor, 121 Reykjavík
New Zealand:
  Pathfinder, 157a Symonds Street, Auckland
Sweden:
  Pathfinder, Vikingagatan 10, S-113 42, Stockholm
United States (and Caribbean and Latin America):
  Pathfinder, 410 West Street, New York, NY 10014

CONTENTS

Ernie Mailhot

A ramp worker and cleaner at Eastern Airlines in Miami and then New York, Mailhot, 42, was a rank-and-file Eastern striker. He was strike staff coordinator for Local Lodge 1018 of the International Association of Machinists (IAM) at La Guardia Airport from December 1989 to December 1990. A socialist since 1970, he has been active in many union and other social struggles.

Judy Stranahan

As a staff writer for the *Militant,* Stranahan, 36, wrote extensively on the Eastern strike. From 1985 to 1990 she was a member of the International Ladies' Garment Workers' Union in Price, Utah, and an active supporter of struggles of the United Mine Workers across the western coalfields. In 1989 she was the Socialist Workers Party candidate for mayor of Price.

Jack Barnes

National secretary of the Socialist Workers Party, Barnes, 51, was won to socialism in the early 1960s by the example of the Cuban revolution. He is a contributor to *Malcolm X Talks to Young People* and the author of *The Changing Face of U.S. Politics,* which charts a course for revolutionary fighters in the trade unions.

Photos, top to bottom: Jon Hillson, Dave Wulp, G.M. Cookson

This book tells the story of the rank-and-file members of the Machinists union at Eastern Airlines. Their twenty-two month strike, which ended when Eastern folded in January 1991, was a frontline battle against union busting that won important gains for all working people.

The Machinists at Eastern faced demands of the bosses (for a massive cut in wages, the gutting of union rights on the job, and more) that amounted to a cold-blooded ultimatum to accept the destruction of their union. If they resisted, the unionists were to be locked out and permanently replaced by nonunion workers. During the previous decade, similar union-busting offensives had been successful again and again.

Rather than submit to the ruthless dictates of Frank Lorenzo, their employer, the members of the International Association of Machinists at Eastern stood their ground and fought back. When Eastern began operating the airline with scabs, the strikers appealed to the labor movement as a whole for support. They picketed, rallied, organized food banks, raised funds, and went out to explain the issues of the strike to other working people. They were able to show that working-class solidarity can prevent the success of even the most determined anti-labor employer.

The ramp workers, cleaners, mechanics, and other Machinists at Eastern scuttled Lorenzo's drive to build a nonunion airline empire. Under the blows of the strike, Lorenzo lost control of Eastern and was forced out of the airline industry altogether. And when the government tried to use its bankruptcy court to openly back Eastern's union-busting efforts, this too proved unsuccessful in the face of the strikers' perseverance.

Finally, after almost two years on the picket line, the

strikers at Eastern forced the once-mighty airline to admit defeat, close its doors, and put its properties on the auction block.

The shutdown of Eastern made headlines. But the real story of the strike cannot be found in the mass-circulation newspapers and magazines or on television.

For the big-business media, the downfall of Eastern was a saga of boardroom meetings, courtroom hearings, stock manipulations, and takeover deals. The union's picket lines were ignored or derided as symbols of a lost cause.

A different approach, however, was taken by the *Militant,* a socialist newspaper published in the interests of working people. The weekly coverage of the strike in the columns of the *Militant* forms the basis for this book.

The vantage point of the *Militant* was that of the union membership. It told about the picket lines, rallies, airport walk-throughs, and other activities that carried the struggle forward. It told about the tours undertaken by union members to explain the issues in the strike and about the solidarity they awakened among workers and farmers internationally.

Strikers found that the *Militant* was telling their story each week. Many sent in firsthand reports to its strike coverage, as did dozens of other correspondents around the world.

Thanks to the tenacity of the Eastern strikers, union busting has been dealt a blow. The Machinists' struggle sent a message to other working people that it is better to stand up and fight for your rights than to passively accept the bosses' dictates. The achievements and lessons of this struggle can therefore become a weapon for working people everywhere.

March 13, 1991

A strike that won gains
for all working people

BY ERNIE MAILHOT

After 686 days on strike against Eastern Airlines, rank-and-file members of the International Association of Machinists (IAM) and our supporters registered the final piece of our victory against the union-busting drive of the employers when the carrier folded at midnight on January 18, 1991.

On that day, as they left work at airports throughout the United States, grim-faced managers and scabs from Eastern Airlines were greeted by strikers from the IAM. This was something these so-called replacement workers had become used to in the twenty-two-month-long strike at Eastern Airlines. But Friday night, January 18, was different.

Martin Shugrue, the government trustee running Eastern, announced the next day that Eastern had "run out of time and resources." After sixty-two years, Eastern, one of the first and one of the largest airlines in the world, was ending its operations.

Eastern strikers from coast to coast, from Puerto Rico to Canada, reacted by calling to congratulate each other and going out to airports to celebrate.

Mark McCormick was one of the Eastern strikers who made his way to New York's La Guardia Airport the night of January 18. "I wouldn't have missed this for the world," he said, as he stood watching management personnel walk out. With a big smile on his face, he suggested to the managers that they "take tomorrow and tomorrow and tomorrow off."

Over the next few hours, strikers and our supporters showed up—many with handmade signs—at rowdy picket lines. The sign I think expressed our feelings the best was the one at the Miami airport that read, "We said we'd last 'One day longer.'"

The big-business press, which for many months had referred to the strike only in the past tense, sent reporters to airports and interviewed strikers. Now they referred to Eastern in the past tense as they interviewed us in the present.

A typical question to strikers was one asked by a *New York Times* reporter: "Why do you seem happy?"

The next day the *Times* answered its own question in an article that said, "The hatred and passions stirred by the long strike of the International Association of Machinists and Aerospace Workers lie at the heart of why Eastern was forced" to park its 170 planes and begin selling its assets.

The twenty-two-month strike of the IAM had defeated Eastern's attempt to create a profitable nonunion airline and set an example for all bosses who want a "union-free environment" if they can get away with it.

To strikers and other working people, the scope of the accomplishments and victories scored in the Eastern strike are measured by what we were up against.

In 1981 U.S. president Ronald Reagan tried to set in motion union busting on a national scale when he broke the Professional Air Traffic Controllers Organization (PATCO). A pattern soon developed of union-busting drives by the employers in major industries, with Frank Lorenzo's destruction of the striking unions at Continental Airlines in 1983 spearheading the assault.

Takeback contracts, permanent replacement workers, and union busting itself became the order of the day. In the airline industry, nonunion airlines were established and strikes, such as that of the Independent Federation of Flight Attendants at TWA in 1986, were crushed.

On March 4, 1989, when we went on strike at Eastern Airlines, we looked back on almost a decade of many more defeats than victories for labor—defeats that more often than not came without a real fight by union members.

We faced Frank Lorenzo, the number one union buster in the United States. We faced government agencies, such as the Federal Aviation Administration, that continually backed Eastern management in the face of massive union documentation of safety violations at the airline.

We faced the federal government and its proven track record of siding with big business, a course backed by the Democratic and Republican parties alike. In Lorenzo's case the cozy relationship between his airline holding company, Texas Air Corporation, and the federal government was well known. One example that we all talked about was that of the judge who presided over the Continental Airlines bankruptcy in the early 1980s. He was later hired by Texas Air for a cushy post. Thanks, Your Honor.

Major metropolitan newspapers including the *Miami Herald, New York Times,* and *Atlanta Constitution* hammered away at us through articles and editorials saying we couldn't win. Many others, including so-called friends of labor in the Democratic Party, agreed. Even many of us thought the odds were long against preventing Lorenzo from succeeding. Despite this, we decided it was time to fight, rather than accept our only other choice: letting Lorenzo destroy our union and set an example for every other boss like him.

When we walked out on March 4, 1989, most of the rank and file of the IAM sensed our strength for the first time. The Air Line Pilots Association (ALPA) and Local 553 of the Transport Workers Union (TWU), which organized the flight attendants, also recognized our strength and our fighting determination. They joined our picket lines. The unity we had achieved between the unions and the pilots' association greatly increased our initial strength, and, in turn, our confidence.

The huge rallies at airports across the United States, Canada, and Puerto Rico—many held in cities with only a few strikers—showed us the broad support and identification our fight had evoked among working people. Many, having gone through years of concession contracts and union busting, saw the fight as their own.

Our unity was crucial to being able to continue the fight even after Lorenzo placed Eastern under bankruptcy court protection five days into the strike. Despite hundreds of promises to the contrary by company officials over the next twenty-two months, Eastern would never emerge from the protection of the court.

It soon became clear to us that the confidence the rank and file had gained as fighters capable of taking on Frank Lorenzo and all his backers was not shared by the union officialdom in the IAM or the AFL-CIO as a whole.

We began organizing to keep our picket lines strong and to reach out to as many other forces as possible to join our fight. At every turn union officials in the IAM and the AFL-CIO attempted to divert us from focusing on the need to organize our strikers and win to the fight broader ranks of labor.

First, the IAM and AFL-CIO officials proposed a militant-sounding shutdown of the railroads to back our strike at Eastern. This tactic, though, was unprepared by the officialdom, both in the rail workers' unions and among working people in general. It would have led to victimizations and given the bosses a handle to turn public support away from us. As soon as the courts placed injunctions against this move, the tough talk disappeared.

The officials then turned their attention to finding a "white knight" to buy Eastern. This was to be the key to defeating Lorenzo. A new owner would make it worth taking even greater cuts in pay and benefits than Lorenzo had demanded, the officials said, in order to keep the "Eastern family" together. News on the ups and downs of each possible buyout became the focus of the officials' attention, rather than where we were carrying out the fight: on the picket line and at rallies and other events.

For many months the officialdom also focused on the bankruptcy court, urging it to appoint a trustee to run Eastern. Another of their proposals on how to fight union busting was for Congress to set up an emergency panel to investigate Eastern. This was pushed especially hard by the ALPA leadership.

All of these focuses had one thing in common: they looked away from mobilizing the power of the ranks of the unions on strike, of the IAM as a whole, and of the broader labor movement.

Our accomplishments are made clearer by seeing the forces arrayed against the rank-and-file fighters of the IAM—from Lorenzo to the federal government—and the obstacle represented by the strategy of the union officialdom.

The unity of the Machinists, flight attendants, and pilots in a major national strike, over a period of eight and a half months, is something that had not been seen in the airline industry before. Winning the support of the pilots for that period of time allowed us to begin to put our stamp on the battle and step forward as a rank-and-file leadership. In addition, we became seasoned enough to understand and weather the later treachery of the pilots' officialdom.

By the time the pilots ended their sympathy strike on November 22, 1989—in the name of saving Eastern and getting on with their lives, as Skip Copeland, the head of the Eastern pilots, said—we in the ranks of the IAM were prepared to continue the fight. We knew that this was not a pilots' strike, as so many tried to say, and that we were the main force Lorenzo had to deal with.

In and of itself, this recognition was a victory. It had come about because for months, rank-and-file fighters in the IAM and some among the flight attendants' union had refused to be diverted from the task of organizing a real battle: day-to-day picketing, expanded pickets, rallies, speaking engagements, and other outreach work that helped show the broad working-class support for our just fight.

The joint work we were able to do with the United Mine Workers, backing its strike against the Pittston coal company through the spring, summer, and fall of 1989, also played a big role in our gaining experience and confidence. From Los Angeles, to Buffalo, to Pittsburgh, to Miami, the striking Machinists and miners learned from each other. Sometimes this took the form of joint tours; other times it meant collaborating to figure out how best to rally support for both our strikes within the unions.

These organizing experiences helped show us that we could affect the battle. The dealings in the courtroom, conflicts among competing investor schemes, and debates in Congress—all these reflected the pressure brought to bear when we exercised union power and reached out to the broader ranks of labor.

Our slogan became that we would last "one day longer" than Frank Lorenzo. This meant that we would never let Eastern run a profitable airline as long as it operated with scab labor. We knew that by achieving that goal, we would help set an example for every other working person in the United States and internationally—our real family, not the "Eastern family." On April 18, 1990, in a victory for all labor, our slogan became a reality.

On that day the federal government, through its bankruptcy court, removed Lorenzo from control of Eastern. He had been heralded as the example for the business class in the United States of how to boost profits by ridding industry of the unions. Yet even with government support and a $400 million war chest, Lorenzo had been defeated. This had been accomplished by several thousand IAM members organized, to a large extent, by rank-and-file leaders who refused to walk away from the fight.

Our strike momentum later showed itself as Lorenzo was forced out of Continental as well—and even that did not prevent Continental from having to file for bankruptcy a few months later, on December 3, 1990.

After Lorenzo was removed, our slogan remained "One day longer," but it became "One day longer" than Eastern.

For more than a year, bankruptcy court judge Burton Lifland did everything possible to back up Eastern management, including giving them the use of the hundreds of millions of dollars in escrow they needed to try to break our strike and somehow become profitable. Lifland now sat in court berating Lorenzo for squandering a billion dollars.

The federal government had tried to avoid stepping directly into the Eastern battle, hoping that Lorenzo would be able to vanquish the IAM as he had the unions at Continental. The fact that this proved to be impossible was a big setback for the employers and their government. The government was forced to appoint Martin Shugrue as trustee to run Eastern, thus openly sharing the responsibility for trying to successfully reorganize the airline and protect Eastern's assets from a simple fire sale.

Finally, on January 18, 1991, after throwing away hundreds of millions of dollars in an attempt to avert such a sale, Martin Shugrue announced that Eastern would be closed. A few days later the IAM announced that on January 24, the 692d day of the Eastern Airlines strike, we would take down our picket lines and mark the official end of the strike.

The main series of victories over union busting at Eastern, though, had been achieved some months before. All that remained to be seen was in what way our accomplishments would finally be registered. It is fitting that Eastern, and its several-year-long crusade against unionism and workers' rights, had to go out of business once and for all.

The fighting Machinists and our supporters accomplished huge things that go far beyond the struggle for the jobs that we had at Eastern. We showed that unlike the Lorenzos and the rest of the boss class in this country, who are motivated by greed for profits, workers will step forward and put themselves on the line in the interests of working people everywhere. This also came through in thousands of examples of other unionists pitching in to support our strike—not only here, but in New Zealand, Britain, Bermuda, and other countries.

The employers' war against working people in the United States continues. Our brothers and sisters on strike against New York's *Daily News* are saying, as we did, that they will stand by the unions as the first line of defense against attacks on our rights and living standards.

Many of us who walked the picket lines at Eastern for more than twenty-two months continue to walk picket lines at the *Daily News* and with other strikers in their fights around the United States and internationally.

Thousands of us are now working in other IAM-organized jobs, as packinghouse workers, as aerospace workers, or in other industries. We take the lessons of the strike with us, and one lesson we will never forget is "An injury to one is an injury to all."

It is important to remember that our fight against Eastern and other companies like it not only improves the relationship of forces for other unionists. It also creates a more encouraging environment for all those who fight against social injustices—from racist attacks to Washington's criminal wars, such as the slaughter recently unleashed against the people of Iraq.

Because of our fight at Eastern, a boss who is considering forcing his workers out on strike so he can break their union and lower their wages and benefits will think a little longer before making such a move.

As important as that is, even more important is the impact we have had on the thinking of working people who are inspired by our fight and will come to follow our example.

As Eddie Camargo, an Eastern striker from La Guardia Airport, said the day after Eastern closed, "I'm very happy this day came. It's been a long twenty-two months, but fighting is the only way. If others follow our example, we'll have strong unions."

We will. In the process we will change the unions into fighting instruments of the rank and file—the engine of a social movement that can transform this country.

'One day longer'
How the Machinists defeated Lorenzoism

BY JUDY STRANAHAN

At 12:01 a.m. on March 4, 1989, 8,500 members of the International Association of Machinists (IAM)—ramp service workers, cleaners, stock clerks, and mechanics—struck Eastern Airlines, a subsidiary of what was then the third-largest airline company in the world, Texas Air Corporation.

Texas Air's primary owner was Frank Lorenzo, who in 1983 had launched a successful union-busting drive at Continental Airlines. His triumph over the unions there was seen as the model by other employers. Lorenzo was determined to add Eastern to his "union-free" Texas Air empire. Instead, the strikers beat back, outlasted, and forced out Lorenzo. In so doing, they defeated one of the point men in the employers' decade-long offensive against labor.

The victories by the rank-and-file Machinists at Eastern make it a more difficult proposition for the employers today to use union busting—or "Lorenzoism" as it was sometimes called—to secure successful, more profitable corporations.

Many in the labor movement today point to the busting of the Professional Air Traffic Controllers Organization (PATCO) in 1981 by the Ronald Reagan administration as one of the opening shots in a broad offensive against the unions in the United States. As part of this offensive, "good-faith negotiations" are dispensed with, and the massive use of scabs as permanent replacements for strikers has become more and more common.

During the PATCO fight the government directly intervened by firing the strikers, who were government employees. In subsequent fights, however, the government has basically stood aside and let the employers go after the unions directly.

Following the defeat of PATCO, it was the breaking of the unions at Continental by that airline's management that prepared the way and became a model for the employers' assault on the unions, not only in the airlines but more broadly.

Frank Lorenzo led this assault. He had acquired Continental Airlines through a takeover in 1982, making it a subsidiary of his Texas Air Corporation. In 1983 Continental's management demanded from its unions a 40 percent wage cut, work-rule changes that would have led to the elimination of six hundred jobs, and other far-reaching concessions. Faced with these union-busting demands, two thousand members of the IAM at Continental went out on strike on August 13 of that year.

Lorenzo moved quickly against the walkout, firing strikers and bringing in scabs. His success in dividing the workers at Continental was registered by the fact that when the strike began, the pilots and flight attendants crossed the IAM's picket lines and continued to work.

Then, on September 24, 1983, Continental filed for bankruptcy, citing "excessive labor costs." Abrogating its contracts with the unions, Continental laid off its 12,000 employees. The airline then rehired 4,200 workers at half their previous pay.

Prior to these moves, Continental's work force had already granted, or had offered to grant, big concessions. The pilots' association had agreed to $100 million in concessions; the flight attendants' union offered up to $90 million over a two-year period. Once the cuts went into effect, pilots' maximum pay dropped from $79,000 a year to $43,000. Flight attendants, who were making $28,000 a year, were offered $15,000.

On October 1, 1983, the Union of Flight Attendants (UFA) and the Air Line Pilots Association (ALPA) at Continental joined the IAM's picket line. But by then it was too late. Lorenzo was able to run a successful and—for the moment—profitable nonunion operation. The unions at Continental had been broken.

Through his success in forcing the unions out on strike, revoking contracts, moving in scabs to permanently replace the strikers, and getting a nonunion operation going, Lorenzo had emerged as the prime example of how employers could break unions in their workplaces—and profit by doing so.

The success of the union-busting drive at Continental was used as a club by other airline owners against workers throughout the industry. At every major unionized airline, including United, Pan Am, and Trans World Airlines (TWA), concessions were demanded by the employers and routinely agreed to by a majority of the work force.

Two days after Lorenzo took Continental into bankruptcy, Frank Borman, president of Eastern at the time, threatened to do the same to his company's workers unless they accepted large pay cuts and other takebacks. The Machinists union, flight attendants, and pilots at Eastern had already granted concessions to Borman the previous several years.

By the end of 1983, the Machinists and flight attendants at Eastern had agreed to an 18 percent pay cut for one year; the pilots, 22 percent. As an incentive to accept the givebacks, union members received new stock the company issued—stock that is now worthless. As part of the deal, union officials were given seats on the board of directors. A year later the company resisted the scheduled restoration of the 18 percent wage cut.

Flight attendants—among the lowest-paid workers at the airline—were hit especially hard by the concessions, which included a multitiered wage system. At the bottom of this new wage structure were the workers based in Latin America and the Caribbean.

In 1986 Lorenzo prepared to further his nonunion airline empire by purchasing Eastern Airlines. Eastern's workers designate this as the beginning of a "reign of terror," consisting of stepped-up harassment and victimization of workers, firings, forced overtime, and speedup. Thousands of union members were either laid off or fired outright in this period.

Lorenzo aimed to destroy the unions at Eastern, just as he had done at Continental, and to make Texas Air—the world's third-largest airline entity—the model for airline employers everywhere.

Many Eastern strikers explained how the 1983 defeat at Continental weighed on them as they entered into the fight with Lorenzo. Moreover, after the walkout at Eastern began, Lorenzo was able to use Continental as a weapon against the strike—through "wet-leasing" planes (leasing the plane and the crew) from Continental to Eastern and having nonunion Continental mechanics and other workers service Eastern flights.

Since the international recession in 1974-75, millions of workers in North America have had first-hand experience with concession contracts, speedup on the job, plant closings, company bankruptcies, the spread of unsafe working conditions, and other aspects of the employers' offensive.

Coming out of its victory in the Second World War, which made Washington top dog in the imperialist world, the employing class in the United States had the latitude to grant gradual concessions to workers. But this ended in the face of a declining profit rate, increased international competition, and the beginnings of a long-term economic crisis following the 1974-75 world recession—problems that have increasingly marked the United States since then.

The superrich U.S. ruling families began a systematic drive to make working people pay for this crisis by squeezing higher profits from their labor. The goal of the billionaire owners of the banks and corporations is to weaken, and where possible destroy, the most important mass organizations of working people—the industrial unions.

In the years following the 1974-75 recession, the bosses launched selective assaults on particular unions. For example, a takeback contract was imposed by the Chrysler Corporation on members of the United Auto Workers in 1979.

The retreat of the unions under the initial blows of this offensive turned into an all-out rout in the wake of the 1981-82 economic recession. Employers in industries where competition had become especially sharp were pressing for deep wage cuts, massive job reductions, big cuts in medical care and pensions, and work-rule changes resulting in deteriorating job safety conditions. In many cases there were three and four separate rounds of concessions. Often the employers' demands posed the question of whether workers should fight or face the possibility of having the union pushed out of the workplace altogether.

In industry after industry and union after union, massive concessions were shelled out to the employers. In the steel industry, for example, the bosses demanded and got big concessions from the United Steelworkers of America in 1983. Additional wage and benefit takebacks were agreed to in the 1986 round of contract negotiations, as well as speedup and the elimination of thousands of jobs. The following year, the entire framework of industry-wide bargaining in steel was broken apart when the USX Corporation imposed a contract that would expire one year later than contracts the union had with other steel companies.

The defeat of the unions at Continental thus came at the beginning of a period in which the union officialdom capitulated to the bosses' demands. Workers saw no perspective for successful resistance. Instead, they often ran away from the fight. Top union officials, along with the companies, promoted the idea that concessions were needed to save "our" company and to make goods produced in "our" state or country more competitive.

Union members went along with and often voted for wage cuts, multitiered pay scales, subcontracting of union work, and temporary-worker schemes that qualitatively deepened the divisions within the work force and among union members.

While affected by the thrashing the labor movement as a whole was taking, the United Mine Workers of America (UMWA) was the only major industrial union in the United States that refused to buckle under to the offensive and give such sweeping concessions. Earlier struggles by the ranks of the UMWA to democratize their union in order to more effectively exercise union power were decisive in their ability to hold off the coal bosses in a hard-fought 111-day strike in 1977-78 and in another major strike in 1981. When the contract expired in 1984, the mine owners backed off and did not demand big takebacks.

But the A.T. Massey Coal Company, one of the largest coal operators in the United States, refused to sign the 1984 agreement between the UMWA and the Bituminous Coal Operators Association, the umbrella association that many coal bosses belong to.

Massey had developed a reputation in coal communities throughout Appalachia as a union-busting operation. The company had successfully opened up nonunion mines in West Virginia and Kentucky in the early 1980s. Massey's refusal to sign the union contract and its decision to impose a substandard agreement forced union members working at the company's mines in southern West Virginia and eastern Kentucky to go out on strike.

Many miners recognized that if Massey were successful in its efforts against the UMWA, this would embolden other coal operators to challenge the union.

The miners at Massey put up a tough fight and mobilized support throughout the union in an attempt to counter the company's hiring of scabs and the operation of its nonunion mines. But as the strike continued, the mobilizations waned. Efforts by the UMWA officialdom to win the fight through court suits and unfair-labor-practice complaints with the National Labor Relations Board failed. In the end the union lost the battle, and Massey was able to successfully run a nonunion coal company.

Nevertheless, the coal bosses' recognition in 1984 that the miners would fight any broad attempt to attack their hard-won gains was the first indication of a growing resistance among working people to the incessant takeback demands of the employers. Workers were beginning to see through the employers' promises that concessions would lead to job security and future wage increases; in fact they led only to more concessions and a weaker union. At this point a series of defensive battles waged by the union movement broke out.

The call to resistance did not come from the top officials of the unions. These "labor statesmen" had shown many times over that they were quite willing to accept concessions demanded by the employers and sell them to the unions' members. But faced with the prospect of a drastic short- and long-term decline in union membership figures—and thus in their dues base—officials in some unions have sanctioned strikes and backed actions to defend their union's very existence.

In the latter half of 1985 members of the United Food and Commercial Workers union (UFCW) began to fight back against the brutal conditions being imposed on them by the bosses in the meat-packing industry. These struggles included the strike of packinghouse workers against Geo. A. Hormel & Co. in Austin, Minnesota, in 1985-86. This was a strike that focused broad nationwide attention on the resistance being offered by the rank and file of the labor movement. Although defeated, this struggle had an impact on unionists across North America and helped inspire a wave of strikes in a number of packinghouses in late 1986 and early 1987.

In 1986-87 in Watsonville, California, cannery workers carried out an eighteen-month strike that scored gains in defending their union against concession demands by cannery bosses. And paperworkers in several regions of the United States waged a hard-fought though unsuccessful sixteen-month strike against the International Paper Company in 1987-88.

Coal operators in the western United States demanded major concessions from union miners in 1986-87. UMWA members resisted with a series of strikes, and in most cases the miners were able to hold their ground. This resistance, in addition to previous miners' battles, played a part in the coal bosses' decision not to take on the miners' union as a whole when the national agreement expired in 1988.

These battles between 1984 and 1988 marked an important shift in the ability of the employers to simply demand and get concessions from workers, often under the threat of plant closings or bankruptcy. Growing layers of workers in the United States were becoming more willing to resist the employers' offensive. While often courageous and determined, however, most of these battles were unable to turn back concession contracts or the hiring of scabs as permanent "replacement workers."

They could not halt the ongoing profitable operation of the company.

❖

By 1988, after over a decade of pay cuts, work-crew reductions, layoffs, and firings, workers at Eastern were ready to fight. They saw this as their only chance to survive the Lorenzo management's reign of terror, an assault that threatened not only their livelihood but their physical safety, and the safety of passengers as well.

In December 1987, the IAM's contract with Eastern had expired. No new agreement had been signed. Under the terms of the Railway Labor Act, which governs the work force at airlines and railroads, the workers at Eastern were barred from striking until after a government mediator declared an impasse. The Railway Labor Act, like other government labor legislation, serves to string out negotiations and tie up workers with restrictive regulations.

For many months leading up to the date of expiration, the company had made demands for huge concessions, including massive pay cuts for all the Machinists union members.

For instance, the wages of ramp service workers, whose top pay was $15.60 an hour, would have been pushed back to $8 within two years. Newly hired ramp workers would have been paid $5 an hour, reaching a top scale of $5.75 after two years. New mechanics would have begun work at a rate of $10 an hour, and the top pay after three years would have reached $12.10. Aircraft service workers and stock clerks faced similar cuts in pay.

Eastern demanded that union members work across established job classifications. The company also wanted the right to lay off employees at will, then rehire some of them as part-time workers; this was part of a plan to establish a new category of part-time employees lacking rights and benefits. A cut in sick pay was also sought. Hoping to split the IAM membership, the company urged the mechanics to negotiate a separate contract.

Responding to these demands the IAM officials called for a federal mediator to help negotiate the dispute. This was agreed to. But Eastern continued to demand $150 million in concessions from the Machinists.

However, workers at Eastern had already endured a decade of concessions, during which they gave $1 billion, by the IAM's estimate, in wage cuts. Now IAM members at Eastern said, "Enough!" In September 1988 the Machinists voted overwhelmingly—7,596 to 90—to reject the company's concession-contract demands.

In February 1989 a government-imposed thirty-day "cooling-off" period went into effect. After sixteen months of deadlocked negotiations, the National Mediation Board called on President George Bush to intervene. This proposal was supported by the IAM officials and the AFL-CIO's top leadership, but was opposed by Lorenzo. Buoyed by his earlier victory against the unions at Continental, Eastern's boss felt confident that his Texas Air Corporation was in good enough shape to defeat the IAM in a strike, and he saw no need for government intervention.

In fact, Eastern had long been preparing for a strike and had amassed a war chest of at least $400 million to finance its drive against the unions. At the same time, it had engaged the services of Continental Airlines in the event of a strike, diverting hundreds of millions of dollars to that carrier, which was, like Eastern, part of Texas Air.

Eastern's owners thought they were well prepared for a strike and made a vow to keep their planes flying—and to do so profitably. They hired armed thugs from private cop agencies to guard company equipment and property and to intimidate the workers. They hired hundreds of workers to act as scabs to replace IAM members and ordered nonunion workers, along with members of management, to perform the IAM members' jobs. Eastern had lined up a hundred management personnel to pilot the planes in the event—thought unlikely—that the pilots honored the picket line. Even in that event, Eastern expected as many as six hundred ALPA pilots to cross the picket line. If this had happened it would have allowed Eastern's planes to get into the air on day one of the strike—their initial goal.

Others did not want the government to step in either. Editorials in the *Wall Street Journal* and *New York Times,* reflecting an opinion widely held in ruling circles, called on President Bush to "stay out of the way." They were confident that Eastern's stockholders could win without open government help, thus maintaining the illusion that the capitalist state is neutral in labor-capital conflicts.

At the same time, some Eastern workers opposed the president stepping in or any further extension of the cooling-off period. After having had their backs to the wall for years, most of them felt they had nothing left to lose. Many were beginning to come to the conclusion that a fight would be necessary to at least hold the line and to defend themselves from further attacks. The stage was set for a showdown.

The strike begins

On the morning of March 3, 1989—just hours before the deadline that would end the cooling-off period—Eastern's management locked out all IAM members, saying it feared "sabotage" of company property and equipment.

At the Miami International Airport, workers were told at 10:30 a.m. that they had five minutes to gather their belongings and vacate the property. Police canine units—summoned beforehand—were brought in to enforce the order.

Union shop stewards arrived and the Machinists

marched together over to the union hall. When another contingent of workers from the maintenance shops joined the march, chants of "We will win, we will win!" went out.

When midnight arrived the picket lines went up, and the strike was on. The union set up picket lines at airports across the United States where Eastern had operations, including its biggest base at the Miami International Airport. Machinists working for Eastern in Canada and Puerto Rico began to staff picket lines as well.

The strike instantly drew worldwide media attention. It was the battle everyone had been waiting for. If Eastern could emerge from this strike as a profitable, "union-free" airline, then Lorenzoism would sweep through other industries with renewed confidence. A new, demoralizing blow would be dealt working people everywhere.

Leading up to the strike, the Air Line Pilots Association had continued negotiations with Lorenzo. It was not clear until the strike deadline whether the pilots and the flight attendants—the latter belonging to Local 553 of the Transport Workers Union (TWU)—would continue to work or would honor the picket lines. As the deadline hit, however, both the TWU and ALPA announced they would honor the Machinists' picket lines, and 3,400 members of ALPA and 5,900 members of the TWU joined the strike.

Immediately, Eastern's operations came to a virtual halt. Prior to the strike, the airline company averaged 1,040 flights a day, carrying about 100,000 passengers. In the first three days of the strike, only 218 planes took to the air, an average of 73 a day.

Eastern workers had served notice to Lorenzo. They had had enough of the reign of terror and had decided to stand their ground and take Eastern on.

"Eastern management refused to negotiate seriously," explained a leaflet distributed on the picket lines by IAM Local 1018 members at New York's La Guardia Airport in the first days of the strike. To the very end, the leaflet explained, the company had continued "to demand the unlimited right to farm out our work, pay cuts as high as 56 percent in some categories, massive work-rule changes, the hiring of part-time workers, cuts in pension benefits, and more." The strikers said that "acceptance of this contract would mean the breaking of our union."

"This is not just a strike," explained La Guardia striker John Walker, who had been a ramp refueler with twenty-one years at Eastern, "it's for the whole labor movement."

With Eastern shut down and the strikers explaining the stakes in their fight to push back Lorenzo's union busting, support poured in. During the first week of the walkout massive rallies were organized, showing the support the Machinists would be able to garner throughout the course of the fight.

In Chicago, where about eighty Machinists were on strike, a mile-and-a-half-long picket line of 2,000 unionists marched through the terminals of O'Hare Airport. Several large rallies were held at Hartsfield Airport in Atlanta, one of Eastern's largest hubs, including one of 4,000. Several hundred picketed Washington National Airport. And 3,000 workers from throughout New England packed the auditorium of the Boston teachers' union hall to show their support.

The twenty-four Eastern strikers in Cleveland were joined by nearly 2,000 unionists at an airport rally, and the twenty-five Eastern workers on strike in Kansas City organized an event of 600.

At Kennedy Airport in New York, 900 members of the IAM at TWA packed three union meetings to discuss how they could back the strike; they then helped set up a large picket line at the airport. Unionists also joined picket lines in Los Angeles, Detroit, Philadelphia, Washington, D.C., and elsewhere.

Miami, the strike center, was the home of 3,900 of the 8,500 Eastern Machinists on strike. Nearly 7,000 strike supporters attended a rally sponsored by ALPA March 7, which was hooked up by video with seven other such events, and 3,000 turned out for an event outside the IAM union hall the next day.

Even among Eastern workers in Miami not covered by union contracts (ticket agents, reservation clerks, and others), a small number expressed their support for the strike by refusing to cross the picket lines—an unheard-of development warmly welcomed by members of the Machinists local there. Such noncontract workers were putting in a lot of overtime before the strike began. Then, early in the strike, Eastern put the noncontract workers on mandatory fifty-hour weeks, but at forty hours' pay, and topped it off by canceling vacations for the rest of the year.

Shortly after the strike started, IAM officials made plans to set up secondary picket lines at Amtrak and other rail lines in New York, New Jersey, Boston, and other areas with heavy commuter rail traffic.

The IAM leadership's goal in calling for the rail pickets was to tie up the commuter railroads and thus force President Bush to intervene in the Eastern strike. On March 5, however, a federal judge in New York barred the pickets, despite their legality under the Railway Labor Act.

Many Eastern strikers had looked to the secondary pickets as a way to expand the impact of their strike. While some rail workers were anxious to show their solidarity by not crossing the proposed picket lines, many more were unaware and unprepared. The officialdom of the rail unions had given verbal support to the plan to shut the railroads down, but there was no serious organizing to back it up. After the court handed down injunctions against picketing the railroads, the Machinists union leadership called on its members to obey the court's decision.

The Eastern strikers refused to be provoked into breaking the court injunctions and held back from setting up the pickets—a move that could have jeopardized the broad public support for the strike and the unity of the strike itself. Instead, they turned their attention toward other ways to broaden the effectiveness of the strike.

The strike at Eastern was sometimes portrayed as a grudge fight between Lorenzo and Charles Bryan, president of IAM District 100, which included the Eastern workers. But in reality it was the Machinists union membership as a whole whose mobilization drove the struggle forward. They started exercising union power to defend themselves from the antiunion drive. They sought to link up with the tens of thousands of unionists and others who had shown during the first week of the strike how much they were inspired by it and saw the fight as their own.

On picket lines, at rallies, speaking to union meetings, and in the media the strikers focused in on their enemy: Frank Lorenzo, Eastern's chief executive. Buttons and T-shirts with a slash through Lorenzo's name became the symbol of the strike, representing the key challenge facing the entire labor movement.

Through keeping up the picket lines and centering their fire on Lorenzo, the strikers kept on the course needed to mobilize their ranks and the broadest number of supporters possible.

On March 9, 1989, five days into the strike, Lorenzo filed for protection under Chapter 11 of the federal bankruptcy code. Thereafter the media shifted its focus from the strikers' rallies and picket lines to the proceedings of the bankruptcy court.

Lorenzo hoped that by getting protection in the bankruptcy court he could restart the grounded airline. Hit hard by ferocious competition in the airline industry, Eastern had already lost millions of dollars in previous years. With Eastern's operations now brought to a halt by the strike, the company's losses were mounting even more.

The carrier's owners were also hoping to get the strikers and working people in general to turn their attention toward the deliberations of the court and away from the strike. They sought to convince workers that decisions about the strike would be made elsewhere than on the picket lines, and that they could not affect those decisions.

Top officials of the IAM, TWU, and ALPA added to this diversion by claiming that the bankruptcy court was where the decisions would be made on Eastern's future. Instead of deepening the mobilization and organization of the Eastern strikers and other airline workers, the officials put forward the view that the judge could be pressured to make decisions favorable to the strikers, such as replacing Lorenzo.

On April 24, in the first of several reorganization plans submitted to the bankruptcy court, Lorenzo said he would reduce the size of the airline by selling off 40 percent of Eastern's planes; selling the carrier's New York-Boston-Washington, D.C. shuttle to Donald Trump for $365 million; and selling off profitable routes—including Eastern's Latin American routes, which American Airlines later bought—and part of Eastern's Philadelphia operations. Lorenzo still hoped to defeat the strike and accomplish his goal of achieving a profitable nonunion airline—even if a smaller one.

The job of the bankruptcy court is a narrow one, more restricted than that of most courts in the United States. Rulings made by the bankruptcy judge are aimed at protecting the social capital—in this case the planes, equipment, computer systems, terminals, and hangars of Eastern—in the interests of a company's owners, creditors, and ultimately the capitalist class as a whole. The court has nothing to do with the interests of organized labor or of working people in general.

The challenge facing the rank-and-file fighters was to see that they could win only by keeping the strike moving forward, by keeping their eyes focused on the picket lines and strike support activities.

While initially many strikers were drawn into following every aspect of the proceedings of the bankruptcy court, this attitude soon dissipated. As rulings came down that went against the interests of the unions, strikers quickly began to learn that the courts were not neutral. The Machinists pressed forward, keeping the strike firm and continuing to win broader solidarity.

Early on, the Eastern strikers were hit with another diversion—the attempt by the IAM, TWU, and ALPA leaderships to seek out a "white knight" to buy the strike-bound airline. According to these officials, the most important goal of the strike was to keep the "Eastern family" together—just without Lorenzo.

Negotiations took place with several big-business figures, including investor and former baseball commissioner Peter Ueberroth and, later, Chicago commodities speculator Joseph Ritchie. In negotiations with Ueberroth, union officials agreed to $210 million in concessions. For his part, Ritchie demanded no less than $400 million in cuts.

Initially, many of the strikers supported bringing in these so-called white knights and adopted a wait-and-see approach to negotiations with them. But as more of the plans for concessions were revealed, strikers began to oppose the idea that the unions should spend their energy on finding a suitable buyer for Eastern. Some started to conclude that a new owner would not necessarily mean a better situation. In the end, negotiations with Ueberroth and Ritchie collapsed and most strikers decided the best thing to do was to continue the fight.

In the process a layer of strikers began to learn that there is no "Eastern family." There is an Eastern family of owners who profit off labor, and an Eastern family of workers who sell their labor power to the owners. They have no interests in common.

The first sale of a major part of Eastern during the strike was real estate speculator Donald Trump's purchase of the Northeast shuttle. A discussion then began on how to maintain the unity of the strike under these new conditions.

This was an important question. The sale of what became the Trump Shuttle posed the problem that some strikers would return to work while others remained on the picket lines, thus weakening the overall fight.

Some strikers pointed out that anything sold should be treated as struck work, and that the picket lines should remain up. However, union officials took down the picket lines at the shuttle in Washington, D.C., Boston, and New York, and on June 7, when the Trump Shuttle started operation, about two hundred strikers went to work there. Initially, they went back without a contract, but eventually a six-month contract that contained some concessions was agreed to; after the six months were up, they continued to work under an expired contract. The decision to take down the picket lines at the shuttle was a major blow to the strike.

Later on, in March 1990, a company-minded outfit— the Aircraft Mechanics Fraternal Association (AMFA)— won a union representation election among the mechanics working at the Trump Shuttle by a vote of 68 to 18. AMFA, which focuses mainly on raiding operations against IAM-organized mechanics, has also campaigned at other airlines. Their efforts, however, have met with only limited success.

AMFA officials seek a return to the heyday of craft unionism. "When you've got a product that is needed, you don't have to be militant," AMFA official Vic Remeneski told the *Atlanta Constitution* in mid-1990. Although mechanics at the Trump Shuttle voted for AMFA, many rank-and-file Eastern strikers saw the association for what it was. They recognized it as a step away from, not toward, a stronger labor movement.

Something new in the labor movement

After the first few weeks of the strike, it was clear that something new had happened in the labor movement. For the first time in the 1980s, a sustained nationwide strike was under way, and it had not been either blunted or defeated by the bosses.

As the ranks of the IAM at Eastern continued to keep their picket lines up and as Eastern's financial losses mounted, many strikers began to get some experience and take initiatives to strengthen the organization and mobilization of the rank-and-file fighters.

Striker Zena McFadden, a member of IAM Local 702 in Miami, wrote in the June 9, 1989, *Militant,* "The strike headquarters is open 24 hours a day, 7 days a week. At any one time there will be from 25 to 100 people in the union hall." Taking measures to meet their needs during the walkout, Miami strikers set up a food bank, a center to dispatch pickets, and a table where strike T-shirts, buttons, hats, and publicity material were available. A thousand bags of groceries were distributed each week.

"No one tells us what to do," an Eastern flight attendant there said. "We just see what needs to be done and do it. We're on strike, and we're an army, an army of labor, and that's how things get done." Strikers in most other centers also set up food banks for the picketers and their families.

In Los Angeles a solidarity rally for Eastern strikers was held June 17, 1989. The strikers campaigned among unionists in the area to build participation in the event. "This strike is about the very existence of the union," the rally leaflet said. "Lorenzo wants to bust it like he did at Continental. Today the fight is at Eastern; tomorrow it could be at any company organized by the IAM—or any union. Now is the time for all of us to join the fight!"

In Washington, D.C., striking Machinists and flight attendants organized two food banks, assisted by the

United Food and Commercial Workers and the Teamsters. Hughie Kelly, an IAM member with twenty-one years at Eastern, pitched in to keep the food bank going. "This keeps me busy through the entire week," he said. Explaining he was new to putting together such an operation, Kelly said, "I helped organize a union picnic five years ago, but that's it."

"It's like a fifteen-round prize fight," another D.C. striker said. "We've taken some blows, but so has Lorenzo. It's surprising—over the last few weeks, our members have stepped up their picketing, and our support is increasing."

When Philadelphia strikers heard that Lorenzo planned to begin flights from that city July 2, 1989, they began organizing an airport rally. "Everybody is watching this strike," one Machinist there said, "even people not affiliated with this union or any union. When you wear your button they ask you how it's going."

At New York's La Guardia Airport strikers began to organize speaking engagements at area unions, explaining the stakes in their fight and encouraging financial donations and participation in daily picket lines.

A fighting slogan emerged, demonstrating the strikers' determination to block the union-busting drive: "One day longer" than Lorenzo.

By far the most significant reinforcement for the Eastern strike came on April 5, 1989, when 1,700 members of the United Mine Workers of America went out on strike against the Pittston Coal Group.

After working under an expired contract for more than fourteen months, UMWA members working at Pittston's coal mines in Virginia and West Virginia had come to the conclusion that a fight was necessary. Pittston was demanding the right to carry out unlimited overtime work, including on Sundays, to eliminate six hundred jobs, and to cut health and safety benefits.

As in 1984 the coal bosses hesitated to take on the entire union, hoping instead to isolate and defeat a section of it. The miners, however, were determined to avoid a repetition of the defeat at Massey. Their resolve to fight was grounded in a widening knowledge of the stakes involved for the entire union in the fight.

For the next eleven months the ranks of Eastern and Pittston strikers joined together to strengthen each other's battles, using union power to push back their respective bosses.

Both strikes received broad support from the labor movement, including the official backing of the AFL-CIO. The fights these workers were waging inspired other airline workers, coal miners, militant farmers, and millions of workers who had been enduring the decade-long antiunion offensive by the bosses.

Miners joined the Machinists' picket lines in front of Eastern terminals and at airport entrances. And striking Machinists visited "Camp Solidarity"—a strike center that UMWA members set up in southwest Virginia, where unionists and others from around the country and throughout the world came to show their solidarity with the Pittston strike.

In late May 1989, Eastern and Pittston strikers began a joint twelve-day tour through southwestern Pennsylvania, Virginia, West Virginia, and eastern Kentucky. On June 11 a huge demonstration of thousands of unionists and others supporting the Pittston and Eastern strikes was held in Charleston, West Virginia.

Two weeks later striking Machinists participated in the Eleventh National Conference of Women Miners, sponsored by the Coal Employment Project, an organization formed in the late 1970s to help women get and keep jobs in the coal-mining industry.

The Pittston employers refused to give in, and the fight

at Pittston soon was taken up by the ranks of the UMWA. Beginning in June 1989 some 44,000 miners went out on strike throughout the eastern coalfields in support of their embattled union brothers and sisters. The walkout, which extended over a six-week period, gave a real boost to the Pittston miners and helped show the resolve of the mine workers to defend their union.

When the miners occupied Pittston's Moss No. 3 coal preparation plant in Carbo, Virginia, on September 17, 1989, Eastern strikers, other unionists, and supporters joined in a solidarity demonstration of several thousand outside the plant. The demonstration continued for more than three days, until the miners complied with a government ultimatum to vacate the plant.

Through a lengthy struggle, the Pittston workers foiled their employer's union-busting drive, returning to work with a new contract in February 1990.

In addition to the solid links established between Machinists and rank-and-file miners, support for the Eastern strike came in from other unionists in the United States and from workers in many other countries. One outstanding expression of this solidarity came from the Bermuda Industrial Union. This union led an eight-month boycott against Eastern to force the airline to cancel its daily flight in and out of Bermuda. Finally, on January 19, 1990, their efforts paid off. The campaign of the Bermuda unions forced Eastern to stop flying in and out of the island. Their fight became an inspiration to the striking Machinists.

Four months into the strike, on the first weekend of July 1989, Eastern added 146 additional flights a day. Prior to that, the strike-bound airline had eighty.

At the heart of Eastern's plan was to resume enough flights with enough passengers on them to make money.

This plan became central to the airline's effort to break the strike and to operate a smaller but profitable non-union airline tied in with Continental.

"To reestablish Eastern as a significant profitable carrier," the *Wall Street Journal* pointed out on July 3, 1989, Lorenzo "needs paying customers. Lots of them. And that's a tall order for an airline that has had more well-publicized trouble lately than any other in recent times."

During July 1989 Eastern's passenger load (the proportion of available seats on each flight that are filled) on the airline's 226 daily flights began to average about 60 percent. Eastern then announced it would have 390 flights a day by August.

When the July start-up was set, a pattern in the strike settled in: with each move Lorenzo made to get the airline going, the strikers would effectively counter by mobilizing their ranks and winning more support.

Eastern's plans to get more planes in the air posed a direct challenge to the strike. "Now is the time for the labor movement to organize an expanded and ongoing mobilization on behalf of the 17,000 workers on strike against Eastern Airlines," explained an editorial in the *Militant* on July 21, 1989. "Such a mobilization is needed to respond to the new stage the nineteen-week-old strike has reached."

"The July 2 start-up by Eastern of 146 more flights represents the biggest challenge the strike has faced since Lorenzo's attempt to restart the Northeast shuttle the weekend after the walkout began," the *Militant* continued.

To meet Lorenzo's attempts at the beginning of the strike to get the Northeast shuttle back into the air, strikers, with the aid of others in the labor movement, had built up the airport picket lines and held demonstrations and rallies. These were successful in turning away potential customers.

With the July start-up, the striking Machinists again

swung into action. Chanting "Union yes, Lorenzo no!" strike supporters in San Francisco held two mobilizations of 300 each at the airport on July 2. In Newark, a crowd of similar size made up of building-trades unionists, communications workers, postal workers, garment workers, and auto workers joined Eastern strikers, marching and rallying for two hours around the airport.

In Chicago, fire fighters, transit workers, government employees, oil workers, electrical workers, steelworkers, and others swelled picket lines.

"A lot of people who came to La Guardia in New York July 2, ready to get on one of the flights Eastern was starting up, simply did not realize we were still on strike," said rank-and-file strike leader Ernie Mailhot, after beefed-up picket lines were organized there to inform passengers of the continuing fight.

Mailhot explained that the strikers were putting out information in Spanish to ensure that Spanish-speaking working people found out about the strike and honored the picket line.

"This is a fight to defend our unions, our wages and working conditions, our dignity. And many Spanish-speaking people—especially those who are working people themselves—can identify with that. They understand what a step forward it will be for all of us if we win this strike," Mailhot said.

At an action of one hundred unionists in Washington, D.C., on June 25, called "Women's Day on the Picket Line," flight attendants' union leader Sandra Palmer asked the rally, "Why should we stand for concessions? We don't owe anyone an apology for expecting to move forward in our lives and in our jobs. The majority of us on strike are not only women, but also heads of families.

"Do we realize our power? We need to remind ourselves of exactly what we have done," she said. "We have shut down Eastern for 114 days. We have brought Frank Lorenzo to his knees."

In response to Eastern's plans to add additional flights to its schedule at the beginning of August 1989, strikers held another round of actions. In Miami, more than 1,300 strikers and supporters from other unions held a walk-through at the Miami International Airport on July 30. Two days later, at the Detroit Metropolitan Airport, 1,000 strikers, unionists, students, and others picketed and rallied.

Several hundred people from over twenty unions picketed at the Los Angeles International Airport on July 29. In Birmingham that same day, 350 unionists turned out for a rally to back both Eastern and Pittston strikers. Strike support actions of hundreds were held in a number of other cities as well. On July 28, more than 1,000 strikers and other trade unionists participated in a New York City Central Labor Council–supported demonstration outside Continental Airlines' mid-Manhattan ticket offices. Throughout the fight at Eastern, the strikers' call for a boycott of Continental, the other major part of Lorenzo's nonunion empire, was heeded by many working people.

These activities were an important response to the challenge laid down by Eastern's owners. And the strength of these actions reminded the traveling public that the strike was still on.

During this time strikers also picketed Eastern scab-hiring sessions across the United States, explaining the strike to those considering crossing the picket line. Strikers and their supporters turned away many who had been lured into seeking employment at Eastern by advertisements promising long-term employment at a "new Eastern."

In order to get the extra flights going, Lorenzo desperately needed additional experienced pilots. During the first ten days of August 1989, at the prodding of John Bavis, then head of ALPA's Eastern division, and with the support of national ALPA president Henry Duffy, enough pilots crossed the picket line to ensure that the flights would get off the ground. Six hundred ALPA members were now working at Eastern. Two hundred management and regular pilots had stayed on the job when the strike started, and 175 to 200 pilots had already crossed between March and July.

The ALPA officials' treachery against the strike led several hundred flight attendants to cross the line as well. These defections hurt the unity and morale of the strike. But because of the Machinists' growing experience, their confidence in having done serious damage to Lorenzo, and the role of the rank-and-file leadership that had been developing over the previous months, the strikers continued to press their fight.

Leading up to and during the strike, rank-and-file Machinists sought unity with the pilots and flight attendants. IAM members made sure to involve these allies in all aspects of strike work and welcomed them on the picket lines, other strike events, and in the strike headquarters.

Unlike the Machinists and flight attendants, however, pilots are a professional layer in the airline industry who have usually identified their interests more with management than with the ramp workers, aircraft cleaners, mechanics, and flight attendants.

Because the pilots' association in the past had virtually always crossed picket lines of the IAM and the flight attendants, these workers were not confident the pilots would join the fight. But the pilots thought they could get more from Eastern's bosses by joining the picket lines, and many stayed out through the first eight and a half months of the strike. The Machinists in turn reached out to the pilots and succeeded in drawing them toward their common fight against Lorenzo.

The Machinists' unity and determination to fight Lorenzo's reign of terror maximized participation from pilots and flight attendants. At the same time, IAM members more and more came to recognize that the true backbone of the strike was the Machinists themselves. This was to become clear to everyone in November, when the officialdom of the pilots' association, followed by that of the flight attendants' union, announced they were ending their sympathy strike and asked Eastern's management to put them back to work.

As Eastern continued to get planes off the ground, the airline's management began to use subcontracting companies to service the carrier's planes and help get Eastern into the air. Some of these companies are nonunion; others are organized by the IAM and other unions.

Eastern hired companies such as Hudson General, Ogden Allied Services, Servair, and others in cities around the country to do jobs previously performed by the strikers—some of which would now be done by fellow IAM members working for these companies.

In Washington, D.C., out of fifty IAM-organized aircraft fuelers working for Ogden Allied Services at National Airport, three-quarters signed a petition protesting having to perform struck work. This action was in response to a leaflet handed out by strikers from IAM Local 796 that explained, "The fight at Eastern has always been crucial for the entire IAM membership. It's particularly critical now because IAM members in Washington, D.C., as well as Miami, Pittsburgh, Boston, and New York are being forced to service scab aircraft in increasing numbers."

An editorial in the August 25, 1989, *Militant* explained, "The move by Eastern to use subcontracting companies organized by the IAM and other unions to service the carrier's restarted flights is a dagger aimed at the heart of the strike.

"This erosion of union strength and solidarity now poses a danger to the Eastern strike as *IAM-organized* companies are being used to do struck work," the *Militant* stated.

Some Eastern strikers sought to meet this challenge by appealing to IAM members to work together in the union to bring a halt to this situation. They pointed to the threat posed to the strike and to the union as a whole when union members carried out struck work. Moreover, a layer of unionists at the subcontracting companies did not want to service Eastern flights.

United action between Eastern strikers and service company workers was hindered, however, by the legacy of years of deals between union officials and the airline and service companies. Efforts toward such united action met with limited success.

This problem highlighted the fact that those working for subcontractors, whether organized or unorganized, make lower wages, have fewer benefits, and are more subject to firings and other arbitrary actions by the companies than those who work at the major unionized airlines. While some workers at the subcontractors were responsive to the strikers, the fact that union officials had paid so little attention to their situation was a hindrance to resolving the problem of these workers having to do struck work.

Today the plight of workers in service companies remains—along with the need for airline unions to organize a serious fight to unionize other parts of the industry.

❖

Despite all his efforts, Eastern Airlines head Frank Lorenzo had failed to break the strike of the International Association of Machinists. While Eastern had planes in the air, the broad support for the strikers among working people kept the airline from being viable.

Through the fight, strikers in local areas had stepped forward, offered suggestions on how to respond to threats to the strike, come up with new ideas on how to continue winning more support, and brought their experiences to other union fights as they broke out.

In mid-August two car caravans of strikers left Miami on a "Journey for Justice" to publicize the strike, visiting dozens of cities from Florida to Massachusetts. They joined hundreds of Machinists and their supporters at the 1989 New York Labor Day march chanting, "What's disgusting? Union busting!" In other cities strikers led off Labor Day weekend marches and spoke at rallies.

Striker Ed Croft in Los Angeles said in a September 29, 1989, interview with the *Militant,* that the "only way to win this strike is on the picket line. We can't depend on the court systems. If they were going to help us, they'd have done it already."

"The strength of the strike is in the picket line," agreed Richard James, also from Los Angeles. "We're few in numbers, but we're going to turn our volume up."

On October 23, 1,500 unionists turned out in Miami for a "human billboard" on the George Powell Bridge to urge travel agents attending the national convention of the American Society of Travel Agents not to book flights on Eastern. Wearing red "Stop Lorenzo" T-shirts and holding signs, strikers and supporters lined the Rickenbacker Causeway.

During these months, strikers in many cities sought to link up with other fights that broke out. From a strike by telephone workers at NYNEX to struggles by garment workers in Los Angeles and hospital workers in New York fighting to defend their union, the Eastern strikers shared their experiences, bolstered picket lines, and publicized their common struggles.

In addition, many strikers participated in political events in the interests of working people. They joined in meetings, rallies, and marches during the June 1990 tour of African National Congress leader Nelson Mandela in the United States and Canada. They also attended pro-

On March 4, 1989, 8,500 Machinists, supported by 5,900 flight attendants and 3,400 pilots, walked off the job at Eastern Airlines.

Above: Picket line in front of the Eastern Shuttle at New York's La Guardia Airport on the third day of the strike.

The strikers and their supporters focused in on their main enemy—Frank Lorenzo, Eastern's chief executive and the most prominent union buster in the United States.

ERNIE MAILHOT

The onset of the strike brought Eastern's operations to a virtual halt.

Top: Ticket counter at La Guardia Airport during early days of the strike.

Bottom: Planes grounded at Miami in early May 1989.

In cities from coast to coast, from Canada to Puerto Rico, picket lines went up and stayed up. Clockwise from bottom left: Miami International Airport; Roanoke, Virginia; Montréal's Dorval Airport; Washington, D.C.'s National Airport; Detroit Metropolitan Airport.

In April 1989, 1,700 members of the United Mine Workers of America went out on strike against the Pittston Coal Group. For the next eleven months Eastern and Pittston strikers joined together to strengthen each other's battles.

Above: UMWA members and supporters block road leading into a Pittston coal plant. Camouflage uniforms became a symbol of the striking miners.

Top: Pittston strikers join Machinists at Martin Luther King Day Parade in Miami, January 15, 1990. Behind miners, at center in white shirt, is Charles Bryan, president of IAM District 100.

Bottom: Thousands of UMWA members and supporters rally outside Pittston's Moss No. 3 coal-processing plant in Carbo, Virginia, during three-day plant occupation, September 1989.

Wherever working people rallied and demonstrated for their rights, it became common to see contingents of Eastern strikers.

Above: At massive Washington, D.C., demonstration for abortion rights, April 9, 1989.

Bottom right: At Martin Luther King Day rally in Atlanta, January 15, 1990.

ALICIA MEREL

The strikers' militancy and determination inspired solidarity from many sources.

Above: Students from Sarah Lawrence College at La Guardia rally, March 4, 1990.

Right: Ottiwell Simmons, president of the Bermuda Industrial Union, speaking at March 3, 1990, Eastern rally in Philadelphia; that union had led a successful fight to shut down Eastern in Bermuda.

MICHAEL CARPER

Barred from picketing inside the airports, Machinists and supporters staged "walk-throughs"— crowds of supporters marching through airport terminals wearing buttons, hats, and T-shirts. Red strike T-shirts became a well-known symbol of the strike.

Above: La Guardia Airport walk-through, March 31, 1990.

Right: Food bank in Miami, June 1989.

As the strike developed, rank-and-file Machinists realized the government was not neutral, but stood squarely behind Eastern's union-busting efforts.

Right: Martin Shugrue, appointed in April 1990 by the government bankruptcy court as Eastern trustee.

Below: Popular strike T-shirt depicts the government's alliance with Eastern management.

JUDY STRANAHAN

SUSAN FARLEY/*NEWSDAY*

Strikers learned first-hand about the role of the police in labor conflicts.

This page: Strikers in Miami are attacked by police as they confront scabs, April 25, 1990. Retired IAM grand lodge representative Bill Schenck, inset, was injured by cops, hospitalized, and arrested.

Facing page: Strike solidarity march and rally at La Guardia Airport, July 14, 1989, which shut down the entrances to Eastern's departures area for several hours.

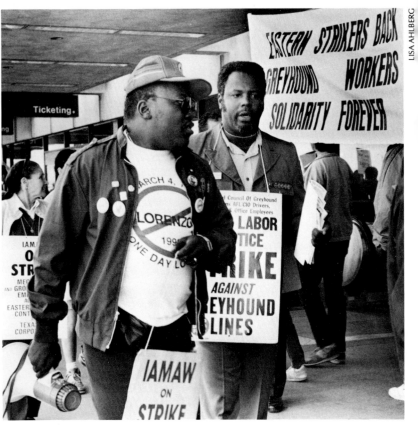

LISA AHLBERG

DON GUREWITZ

Eastern strikers sought to link up with other union battles. Top: Greyhound strikers join Machinists at Los Angeles picket line, March 17, 1990.

Bottom: Striking telephone worker from NYNEX at Eastern strike rally at Boston's Logan Airport, October 12, 1989.

Top: Members of International Ladies' Garment Workers' Union on strike at Domsey Trading Company participate in human billboard at La Guardia Airport, August 4, 1990.

Bottom: Eastern strikers join picket line at New York's *Daily News.*

By staying out "one day longer" than Lorenzo and Eastern, the rank-and-file Machinists scored lasting gains for all working people.

tests in defense of a woman's right to choose abortion, for affirmative action, and around many other issues.

Into the second year: Eastern on the ropes

"The Machinists on strike at Eastern Airlines have reached a new stage in their fight against Texas Air Corporation chairman Frank Lorenzo. Like hardened soldiers pausing to survey their smoke-filled battlefield, the strikers have arrived at the eleventh month of their fight to find their enemy staggering and wounded," began an editorial in the January 19, 1990, *Militant.*

In 1989, Eastern's acknowledged losses were $852.3 million—a record for the airline industry. Despite heavy fare slashing throughout the strike, Eastern's planes were half-filled, and its passenger load factor was dropping. The carrier did not emerge from bankruptcy with a profitable nonunion operation as it had vowed to do by the year's end.

By the first anniversary of the strike, March 4, 1990, the extent of the damage done to Eastern's plans was clear. And the identity of Lorenzo's nemesis was now equally clear: the rank-and-file backbone of the IAM Eastern strike. At events and rallies around the country thousands of strikers and their supporters celebrated 365 days on the picket lines. Just over a month later the full scope of Eastern's troubles, which had been mounting steadily, would become more widely known.

In early 1990 Lorenzo had presented yet another plan to the bankruptcy court for review. The plan included a proposal to pay Eastern's unsecured creditors only 10 cents on the dollar they were owed—but they were owed $1 billion! Lorenzo told the creditors that such fire-sale prices were the best he could do for them. Among these unsecured creditors were Eastern's unionized workers, who never received their last paycheck.

In early April the creditors said no to the deal and on April 18, 1990, bankruptcy judge Burton Lifland removed Lorenzo from Eastern's day-to-day operations. The creditors saw that every day the strike continued the value of Eastern's saleable assets declined. They believed they could do better than Lorenzo's offer, and would be better off without him.

Lorenzo, who had been the darling of the employing class a half-decade earlier, exited from Eastern a pariah—even for paragons of antiunionism like the *Wall Street Journal*.

This was the major turning point in the strike. For over a year the rank-and-file fighters had waged an effective strike and forced Eastern to lose close to a billion dollars. Although they were not able to keep the airline shut down, the strikers had indeed stayed out "one day longer." And in the process they had put an end to Lorenzo's long-term plans to build a profitable nonunion airline empire. This victory sent a message to employers that their ability to simply force workers out on strike, bring in a scab work force, and drive the unions out altogether had been dealt a big blow.

Strikers and their supporters celebrated the victory and turned their attention to the next stage of the fight.

When he ousted Lorenzo, Judge Lifland appointed Martin Shugrue to head up Eastern as trustee acting on behalf of the bankruptcy court. Shugrue's appointment showed that the government was being drawn more openly and directly into the fight at Eastern. The airline's owners had been wrong; they could not win the strike on their own, under Lorenzo's leadership, while keeping the government on the sidelines. Thus the battle took on a more openly political character.

Shugrue hoped to put Eastern's profit-and-loss statement in the black—or at least hold the airline together long enough to find a buyer. His efforts on behalf of the government were a last-ditch attempt to prevent the further bleeding of Eastern through operating losses and to garner for the creditors as much as possible of what they were owed.

To buy some time Shugrue held a few meetings with the union, trying to get the strikers to back off. Initially the union's top officials portrayed Shugrue as someone they could work with. This was never true. The Eastern strikers were now up against the court and government even more directly. The stakes in the fight were raised and broader challenges were posed for the strikers. They continued to press their fight through mobilizations, picket lines, and rallies. With Lorenzo out, the strikers added a new slogan on picket signs and buttons: "No contract, no peace!"

❖

During the summer of 1990, Northwest Airlines expressed interest in buying Eastern. Northwest chairman Alfred Checchi and Shugrue held discussions; IAM officers also met with Checchi. The Machinists union represents 24,000 Northwest workers.

The anticipation of a possible buyout generated a discussion both among union members at Northwest and strikers at Eastern. Some unionists at Northwest raised concerns over seniority should the striking Machinists from Eastern come to work there. But others were sympathetic to the Eastern strikers. Key to the discussion was the need to recognize that if strikers got union jobs at Northwest, this would mark a victory in the strike, resulting in a stronger union for all the workers.

Due to intensified competition among the airlines going into the fall of 1990, however, coupled with a rise in jet fuel prices, Northwest Airlines backed off from its offer to buy a large part of Eastern and opted instead to submit a bid to the bankruptcy court for a much smaller portion of the company. Other airlines also put in bids to buy up parts of the ailing carrier.

Demoralized by Lorenzo's departure, the continued financial bleeding of the airline, and widespread talk about buyouts, members of Eastern's scab work force began to quit the deteriorating operation. Promised long-term employment at a reorganized, growing, and prosperous airline, those who had crossed the picket line recognized that their future at Eastern was indeed shaky. This recognition extended to the top levels of management, where 76 out of 190 left the company.

Eastern received another blow on July 25, 1990, when the company and ten of its management personnel were slapped with a sixty-count criminal indictment for safety violations and failure to maintain the company's planes properly, conspiracy to defraud the government, obstruction of justice, and more. Eastern thus became the first U.S. airline in history to be criminally indicted.

The Machinists union has explained numerous times that the question of safety is of vital interest to the union. "One of the main reasons we did go on strike was that the infractions of safety that we brought out to the company and to the FAA [Federal Aviation Administration] were being ignored and being made a mockery of," said Frank Ortis, national Eastern strike coordinator and president of IAM Local 702 in Miami. The striking Machinists had taken up this important question for all working people— safety in the air—and made it an issue in their strike. The indictments vindicated their efforts. Eastern was now branded a criminal as well as a scab-herder.

Then, in another major victory for the strike, Lorenzo announced on August 9, 1990, that he was stepping down as chief executive of Continental Airlines Holdings Inc. (previously known as Texas Air Corporation) and was selling most of his stake in the holding company to

Scandinavian Airlines System (SAS). As part of a $30 million buyout, Lorenzo agreed to stay out of the airline industry for at least seven years. Frank Lorenzo, the man who set out to rule the airline industry, was thereby tossed onto the scrap heap of failed airline employers. As the news reached the strikers, spontaneous celebrations were held on the picket lines and in the strike organizing centers.

In September 1990, eighteen months into the strike, Eastern missed the deadline for a $95 million payment to the government's pension fund agency, the Pension Benefit Guaranty Corporation. The agency temporarily covered the pension plan, although it could have begun to place liens against Eastern and Continental. An agreement was reached between the agency and Continental Airlines Holdings Inc. making the parent company liable for up to $680 million in payments.

Under the agreement, Eastern would put in only $30 million to cover the pension plan, and the holding company would be allowed to put up $500 million in collateral for the rest of the deficit. Continental was more and more being drawn into the battle and being drawn down by it. Continental's involvement increasingly posed the possibility that union sentiment could take root and union organization could spread among that airline's workers.

Going into October 1990, the nineteenth month of the strike, Eastern's load factor hit a low of 44 percent. Shugrue stated that given the increase in jet fuel prices since the onset of the Mideast crisis in August, Eastern would have to fill its planes to 102 percent of capacity to break even.

New allegations of continued safety violations by the airline were being investigated by the Justice Department. On December 1, federal agents raided Eastern's Miami headquarters and seized safety logs. This was done because of widespread evidence the government had received proving that massive safety violations at Eastern continued under Shugrue.

On November 13, 1990, Eastern management revealed the airline had lost $252.8 million in the third quarter, bringing the total so far in 1990 to $424.9 million. That announcement came as Eastern trustee Shugrue was asking the bankruptcy court to release an additional $30 million from the escrow accounts to keep the airline operating through November. The court instead granted only $15 million.

Then on November 27, the court gave Shugrue $135 million out of the escrow accounts to keep Eastern afloat. Many of the company's creditors were ready to liquidate the airline in order to get some of their debt repaid, even if it meant at fire-sale prices. But the government—through Shugrue—was running Eastern on behalf of the capitalist class as a whole, not just individual ones like Lorenzo or those on the creditors' committee. Giving out more money to keep the airline running was done to protect the interests of capitalism as a whole, in the hope that Eastern could eventually be divided up to the benefit of the entire airline industry—an industry in deep crisis. In the process, the government hoped to undercut the victories the rank-and-file Machinists had already won.

The strikers showed their anger and determination against the court's decision by organizing a march of six hundred strikers and supporters around the airport in Miami on December 1. Other strike centers held activities as well. Banners proclaiming "One day longer!" were kept flying around the country.

On December 3, 1990, Continental Airlines Holdings Inc. filed for Chapter 11 bankruptcy protection. Continental was not merely a casualty of the increased competition and economic crisis in the airline industry. It had also turned up the loser—not the winner—in Texas Air's grand plan against its employees.

Accomplishments of the rank and file and gains for the labor movement

The perspective of the top labor officialdom, including that of the IAM, has always been to seek cooperation between labor and management. At Eastern, however, the IAM officials were caught between a management that was unwilling to cooperate and a work force that refused to go down without a fight.

The officials looked to the bankruptcy court, buyouts, and government intervention as the way forward for the strike. As this focus quickly proved ineffective, rank-and-file members stepped forward with ideas in local areas on how to keep up daily picketing, build rallies, extend solidarity, and win financial support. They began discussing the necessary actions and came up with the tactical moves needed at each stage of the battle.

These initiatives by the strikers demonstrated the extent to which they had moved into the void created by the IAM top officialdom's inability to organize an effective fight.

As the months passed, rank-and-file leaders came to be recognized by a much broader layer of battle-tested fighters. The ranks had sufficient time to find ways of organizing and structuring themselves to keep advancing the strike.

The ranks strived at all times to maintain maximum unity while seeking broader solidarity from other unions and working people as a whole. They weathered many blows and surprises, and in the process they outlasted and defeated their employer—Frank Lorenzo—the man looked to by employers everywhere as the model union buster.

As the months rolled on, many strikers found work at other airlines and other jobs while continuing their picket duty or participating in strike events. In these new workplaces some strikers have drawn on their experiences in the battle at Eastern in an effort to strengthen the unions they now find themselves in.

❖

The achievements of the striking Machinists at Eastern have greatly improved the prospects for all workers to fight back against attacks on them and their unions.

Over the last decade, the U.S. working class and labor movement have suffered heavy blows from the employers' assault. The unions have been further weakened by the class-collaborationist course of the labor officialdom. Indeed, the conviction of the top labor officialdom that working people and the employers have similar interests has only deepened during these years.

However, the labor movement has not been defeated. It has not been shoved out of the center of politics in the United States. Working people continue to demonstrate their capacity for organized resistance.

Battles today, like the one at Eastern, are defensive in character, waged by workers with their backs against the wall. Such fights are being conducted by a layer of workers who have been made desperate by the bosses' attacks on their standard of living and working conditions, and feel they have nothing to lose by fighting. The outcome of these fights has been varied—many substantial setbacks or defeats, some standoffs, and victories in a few cases.

Despite the difficulties and blows, growing numbers of workers and unionists in the United States have found ways to fight. They have sought ways to avoid entanglement in red tape. They have done so even when the bosses and labor bureaucrats have combined to block them from using standard union tactics of organizing their union power and solidarity to shut down production.

In the face of every obstacle, workers have fought back, organized strikes, won the support and solidarity of other working people, and slowed down the impetus of the employers' offensive.

One example of such resistance to the employers' attacks has been the 1990-91 strike by newspaper workers against New York's *Daily News*.

In 1982 and 1987 unions at the *Daily News* had granted the newspaper's owners tens of millions of dollars in concessions. These gains only sharpened the employers' appetite. By the fall of 1990 they had prepared for a showdown that they hoped would break the power of the unions at the *News* and restore the ailing newspaper to profitability.

On October 25, 1990, management swiftly and brutally locked out the workers. Within minutes, scab workers were in place. Armed company thugs were on the scene to intimidate pickets. A scab edition of the paper was printed and shipped that same day.

Yet something happened to upset the employers' well-laid plans. Working people by the thousands declined to buy the scab paper, persuaded their friends not to purchase it, and prevailed on newsstand owners not to sell it.

Five months later, after pouring tens of millions of dollars into their war against the unions, the owners of the *News* had still been unable to restore the paper to its former circulation and were losing three-quarters of a million dollars a day.

The setback delivered to the owners of the *Daily News* required the actions of tens of thousands of unionists and other working people. Such solidarity can play a crucial role in labor and social struggles to come.

Sharp battles lie ahead. On January 16, 1991, the U.S. government opened up a savage, brutal war against the people of Iraq. Using the Iraqi regime's August 2, 1990, invasion of Kuwait as a pretext, Washington had sent

U.S. troops, reserves, and war matériel into the region, taking the necessary time to militarily and politically prepare for an armed assault. By early February 1991, several weeks into the war, the U.S. government had over half a million troops there, making this the largest U.S. troop deployment since the Vietnam War. Britain, Canada, France, and other countries sent troops as well. The combined military forces arrayed against Iraq totaled three-quarters of a million.

Along with the buildup of troops came warships, nuclear-powered submarines, tanks, heavy artillery, aircraft carriers, and warplanes.

As part of its war offensive, Washington—with United Nations backing—imposed on Iraq the most severe economic blockade directed against any country in this century. Backed up by military force, the sanctions even barred medical and food relief.

With the support of the U.S. Congress and the United Nations, the rulers in Washington began their war by raining bombs on the Iraqi people, killing thousands. They then launched their invasion of Iraq, slaughtering tens of thousands of Iraqi soldiers, many of whom were fleeing the U.S.-led assault.

Bush stated that this murderous war was needed to restore sovereignty to Kuwait. But the true aim was to help secure U.S. imperialism's domination over the region's resources by installing a protectorate in Iraq, a regime that would be dependent on U.S. support and subservient to Washington's dictates. By accomplishing this, the U.S. ruling rich also hope to gain an edge over their imperialist competitors—Germany, France, and Japan in particular.

"The patriotic appeals and anti-Arab propaganda of the imperialist war makers are preparing the way for attempts to further curtail our democratic rights," explained Ernie Mailhot.

"After twenty-two months on strike, many of the rank-

and-file Machinists are much more skeptical of what the government tells them. Frank Lorenzo was backed up by the government and backed up by the courts, and Shugrue was a government appointee. This has helped to open up the eyes of some of those who have been on strike at Eastern."

The war takes place as the world capitalist economy is heading toward a depression. This economic crisis has its roots in the never-suppressed capitalist business cycle. It is intensified by declining profit rates, stiffening international capitalist competition, the mounting debt of the Third World countries, the growing banking crisis, and the collapse of the real estate boom. By late 1990 top U.S. government officials had been forced to admit that a recession in the United States had begun.

Already, working people have found themselves in the middle of another kind of war: an onslaught against their standard of living and working conditions. As the economic crisis deepens, the ruling families will seek to squeeze workers and farmers even more, driving down the standard of living, cutting back on social benefits, and trying to gut the union movement. The result will be deepening misery in the working class and accelerated social differentiation.

On January 18, 1991—twenty-two months after the strike started—Eastern Airlines announced it would stop flying at midnight. The next day, Martin Shugrue stated that the airline had "run out of time and resources." Eastern's planes were returned to their hubs and parked. Thousands of passengers were stranded. Airline companies, including Delta, Northwest, and United, scrambled to pick up remnants of Eastern.

With Lorenzo and Shugrue's plans lying in ruins, the striking Machinists had scored a number of victories, which stand as gains for the entire labor movement.

The Eastern strikers succeeded in winning what they could, given the possibilities open to them. They prevented Lorenzo from realizing his goal of building at Eastern the kind of nonunion operation he created at Continental in 1983. In fact the striking Machinists drove him out of the airline industry altogether.

The Machinists' twenty-two month fight played a role in driving both parts of Lorenzo's former Texas Air empire—Eastern and Continental—to bankruptcy. As a result of their fight the government was forced to step in and take direct responsibility for Eastern's future, overriding the wishes of its stockholders and creditors. Ultimately, the strikers forced the nonunion carrier out of business. All this has made other employers everywhere less confident that the open union busting of the mid-1980s is the way to get higher profits today.

The bosses continue to demand takeback contracts, and the employers, their government, and the Democratic and Republican party politicians continue to press their drive against the labor movement. However, the successful battle by striking Machinists against Eastern has provided inspiration for other rank-and-file unionists that they too can mount a resistance to the bosses' attacks.

The strikers fought not just for themselves but for all of us. The victories of the rank-and-file Eastern strikers make Lorenzoism less attractive to employers today.

As Eastern's grounded planes were put on the auction block, strikers all over the country celebrated the final demise of the carrier. Contrary to all their detractors among the ruling rich, the Machinists at Eastern had indeed stayed out "one day longer."

Capitalism's march toward war and depression

BY JACK BARNES

The following is a section from "The Working-Class Campaign against Imperialism and War," published in *New International 7*. It is based on talks originally presented in late November and early December 1990.

T he same week in November 1990 that the United Nations Security Council adopted a U.S.-sponsored resolution authorizing war against Iraq, top U.S. government officials were finally forced to admit that the recession already unfolding in Canada had also begun in the United States.

It was also the same week that the federal government announced that for the fourth year in a row the average life expectancy of Black people in the United States had *declined*—declined in absolute terms. That decline was large enough to result in a drop of the overall average life expectancy in the United States. Moreover, this decline has been very class-divided. It results from rapidly deteriorating health conditions among the worst-off layers of the working class, not limited to those who are Black.

The very fact that average life expectancy can drop in the last decade of the twentieth century in the world's wealthiest imperialist power—and that it can decline for four years in a row for working people from an oppressed

nationality—is a sign of the depth of the underlying capitalist economic crisis. Driven to reproduce the social relations of production necessary for its own existence, capitalism is regenerating and extending the institutions of
racist oppression. This process intensifies the exploitation of working people as a whole and deepens class
polarization.

Behind this statistic lie many others, and all of them
point to the truth about what is coming, about the character of the international social crisis we are heading into
and the stakes for working people in the battles that lie
ahead. We can't predict the exact timing or how events
will unfold, but we can say with certainty that the imperialist ruling classes today are marching workers and
farmers toward war and depression.

As the working class in the United States goes into the
current recession, it has already been the victim of a more
than decade-long offensive by the employing class against
our living and working conditions. Workers' real wages
dropped by 8 percent in the 1980s. In fact our buying
power has dropped so sharply that it is now at the same
level as in 1961. Since 1980 our pensions, health benefits,
and insurance protection have dropped about 15 percent
on average in real money terms. As a result of the pres-
sures from this assault on workers' incomes, the debt
burden on working-class families has skyrocketed as they
desperately seek to somehow buffer the blows to their
living standards.

With unemployment already rising sharply, only one-
third of those out of work in this country are currently
receiving jobless benefits, largely because of major government slashes in the form of stiffer eligibility require-
ments. This contrasts to more than three-quarters of jobless workers during the 1974-75 recession and about half
during the deep capitalist downturn in 1981-82.

Working farmers are in for another round of accelerat-
ing indebtedness, bankruptcies, and foreclosures. The

capitalist farm crisis that drove tens of thousands of exploited producers off the land in the early and mid-1980s—the worst times since the 1920s and '30s—is far from resolved.

The capitalists are weighed down under an enormous debt structure that reached historic heights during the 1980s. Investment in new, capacity-expanding plant and equipment stagnated throughout the decade. Meanwhile, there was an explosion of real estate speculation, debt-financed buyouts and mergers, and junk bonds, plus growing instability on the stock and commodities markets. The Third World debt continued to climb to staggering levels, devastating the workers and peasants in those countries and putting new strains on the imperialist banking structure. The banks, savings and loan institutions, and giant insurance companies in the United States—as well as the funds today available to government agencies that supposedly protect depositors and beneficiaries—are in their weakest condition in many decades.

Sudden breakdowns or partial crises on any one or more of these fronts—all of which are more vulnerable given today's capitalist downturn—threaten to turn a recession into a collapse of the international banking system that can plunge the world into a major depression and social crisis.

Antilabor offensive

The employers, their government, and the Democratic and Republican party politicians continue to press their anti-working-class, union-busting offensive. The ultimate solution to all the country's economic problems, they insist, is to guarantee workers the "right" to work in a "union-free environment." More and more they act as if the only good worker is a "permanent replacement" worker.

The bosses continue to demand takeback contracts—such as the recent pacts accepted by the United Auto Workers officialdom—that deepen divisions in the working class by agreeing to trade off wages, conditions, and job opportunities for younger workers and new hires in return for the will-o'-the-wisp of "job security" for a declining number of higher-seniority union members. The employers continually push to gut health and pension benefits, speed up production with less union control over safety on the job, and ravage the environment.

City and state governments around the country—as in the mid-1970s—are complaining of "declining tax revenues" and "tightening budgets," and "reluctantly" point to the need to sharply cut the rolls of public employees and impose takeback contracts. Governors and mayors are slashing expenditures on basic health services, education, child care, and other social programs that millions of working people depend on. Bridges and roads continue to deteriorate dangerously.

So workers and farmers in this country face a double march today: a march toward a horrible war; and a march not only into a recession but toward a seemingly inexorable worldwide depression and social crisis.

This reality is sensed by growing numbers of working people. And it poses big challenges and responsibilities for every thinking worker, every rank-and-file union militant, every communist.

Labor movement not pushed out of politics

The U.S. working class and labor movement have suffered blows; our unions have been further weakened by the class-collaborationist and proimperialist course of the labor officialdom; and we have been put on the defensive by the accelerated onslaught of the employers in the 1980s.

But we have not been defeated. The labor movement has not been shoved out of the center of politics in this country. Our capacity to resist has not been broken.

Since the middle of the 1980s, as resistance by the working class and unions in the United States has evolved, a pattern has emerged. Despite the difficulties, despite the blows, workers and unionists in the United States pushed to the wall by the employers' assaults have found ways to fight. Layer after layer of workers have managed to avoid simply being handcuffed, chained, and prevented from organizing to defend themselves. They have done so even when the bosses and labor bureaucrats have combined to block them from using standard union tactics that have brought victories throughout the history of the labor movement—that is, even when they are blocked from organizing union power and solidarity to shut down production.

As workers have moved into action in the face of these odds, other working people have expressed solidarity with their battles. Important experiences with rich lessons on how to forge unity, overcome divisions, and wage an effective struggle have begun to be accumulated by a small vanguard of fighters in the labor movement. These defensive efforts are waged from a position of weakness. The ranks are not in a strong enough position to push aside the current labor officialdom and replace it with another leadership that has an alternative, class-struggle strategy. Their efforts have to take place largely within the limits of the strategy imposed by this ossified bureaucracy. But this fact makes these experiences no less important as the arena where rank-and-file fighters find each other and test each other.

All this is being experienced right now as the *Daily News* strike unfolds in the greater New York City area.

This is a strike that began in October 1990 as one of the most cold-blooded, brutal, militarily organized lockouts by management in years. The union officialdom hoped against hope that this fight would not happen. As a result, the ranks of the drivers, press operators, and other unionized employees were forced into a fight without any preparation. The ranks have no democratic union structures through which to organize, make decisions, argue out tactics, strive for greater unity among themselves, and reach out for broader solidarity from the rest of the labor movement—in order to bring their real potential power to bear.

Management, on the other hand, was well prepared. Production never stopped. The *Daily News* didn't miss a single edition. It had scabs lined up months in advance to do everything from writing copy, to typesetting and printing the papers, to transporting them throughout the metropolitan area. The scabs were at their posts within a matter of minutes—together with armed thugs to go after the unions. The rest of New York's big-business media joined in the company's violence-baiting of the unions.

But then something happened that management had not anticipated. They could write the paper, print the paper, and truck the paper with "permanent replacements." But they couldn't get working people to buy it! The working class in the New York area pulled together to keep the *Daily News* off the newsstands. They put pressure on the owners of the newsstands they patronize not to carry the scab paper; they argue with them, try to convince them. Some of these small shopkeepers have put up solidarity signs announcing, "We don't carry the *Daily News.*"

Workers argue with co-workers on the job and with friends and family members not to buy the paper. They've made buying the *Daily News* an immoral, rotten, unconscionable act for any working person with an ounce of decency, human feeling, and solidarity. Unionists have volunteered to go out and ring doorbells to urge people to cancel their subscriptions.

There are thousands of retail outlets that carry daily

newspapers in greater New York. Prior to the strike, the *Daily News* was the second-largest-selling metropolitan daily in the country. Yet, today it's difficult to find a newsstand that carries it. This was not accomplished by centralized organization. It took the actions of tens of thousands of workers and unionists. Newsstand owners found that carrying the *Daily News* was considered an insult by regular customers—people they've gotten to know, made friends with, depend on for steady business. These kinds of factors play a role in labor and other social struggles, and they are having a big impact on the *Daily News* strike.

The point here is not to try to predict what the outcome of this strike will be, given the character of the officialdom in these unions and the overall state of the labor movement. To keep moving forward against the *News* management, space must continue to be opened by the printing trades officialdom for the ranks to operate, and the ranks must have time to find ways of organizing and structuring themselves, as we saw happen in the Eastern Airlines strike.

The entire working class feels a growing hatred for the antiunion assault, and this enables strikers like those at the *News* to gain increased solidarity from other unionists and workers. As a result, even if the strike does not have the ability to shut down production, some unexpected space is opened up for it. But other expressions of struggle and solidarity are not a substitute for the strike; they are a supplement to it. They become a way for the ranks to assert themselves and prove that union busting is not a sure winner for the bosses. All this is very important right now and deserves the active support of all workers, regardless of the duration or expected outcome of the effort.

The *Daily News* strike is just the most recent example of the pattern that has emerged from the labor struggles in this country in recent years. It is an uneven pattern, one with gaps and breaks. But the pattern is nonetheless clearer today than when it began to take shape back in August 1985 with the strike of the packinghouse workers against the Hormel Company and other battles in meatpacking over the following eighteen months to two years.

Since then there have been other fights: by paperworkers, by cannery workers, by coal miners in both the eastern and western fields, by telephone workers, by hospital employees. All have been defensive in character, waged by workers pushed deeper and deeper into a corner by the employers. They've had various outcomes: some substantial setbacks or defeats, some standoffs, a few victories. The most weighty victory in the recent period has been that won by members of the United Mine Workers of America and their supporters against the union busting of the Pittston coal company. The UMWA remains the most formidable single obstacle to the employers' hopes.

But through all these fights you can watch not just the cumulative impact of the assaults, but also the cumulative effect of workers finding ways to resist for slightly longer, or surprising the employers a bit more with what they are able to accomplish, and thus giving greater confidence to other layers of the working class who will find themselves in struggle.

The strike by members of the International Association of Machinists against Eastern Airlines that began back in March 1989 has been a little different from the rest. There, through the initial months of the battle, a rank-and-file leadership of the strike came forward and had enough time to structure itself. It kept reaching out to maintain maximum unity while drawing in broader solidarity from elsewhere in the labor movement. These strikers demonstrated the capacity to take the blows and withstand the shocks that came their way and to outlast and outfight the employers. And it was not your run-of-the-mill boss they were up against. Frank Lorenzo was the man the employing class considered the union buster of the decade, a model for them all.

The Eastern strikers blocked Lorenzo from imposing on them the kind of nonunion operation he had rammed down the throats of workers at Continental Airlines in 1983. In fact, the IAM strikers drove Lorenzo out of the airline industry, and their nearly two-year-long fight has brought both parts of Lorenzo's former Texas Air empire—Eastern and Continental—to bankruptcy. They have made the government step in and openly take direct responsibility for Eastern's future—to the horror of its individual stockholders and creditors. This has made other employers, suppliers, and bankers—inside and outside the airline industry—less confident that blatant union busting, "Lorenzoism," is the high road to high profits that it seemed to be in the mid-1980s.

The labor movement is not on the offensive against the employers. There are no developments anywhere in the unions that represent the organized beginnings of an alternative, class-struggle strategy. The labor movement is still being weakened by the class-collaborationist course of the officialdom in the face of the rulers' continuing offensive. All that is correct.

But that is not the entire story. The pattern of resistance by workers and unionists over the past half-decade, the search for ways to bring class solidarity to bear, the openness to reaching beyond themselves, beyond the union movement, beyond the country to seek and extend solidarity—these facts, too, have to be brought into the picture. And they are among the decisive facts on the basis of which communist workers, who are part of this working-class vanguard, must chart our strategy and tactics—including in campaigning against the imperialist war drive.

Independent working-class political action

These struggles bring a vanguard layer of workers additional experience that makes them more open to seeing themselves as part of a class with interests different from and opposed to the employers, the employers' political parties, and the employers' government. The unity workers have needed to forge in order to advance their own fights, and the solidarity they have reached for, helps clear away some of the divisions and reactionary prejudices promoted by the employers. This increases the capacity to recognize common interests with other working people both in this country and around the world.

These shifts are important for communist workers, because they provide new opportunities—grounded in common experiences of rank-and-file union militants—to win broader understanding of the need for a labor movement that operates on the basis of democracy, class solidarity, and independent working-class political action. A labor movement is needed that rejects the narrowness of unionism as conceived by a timid officialdom. A fight is needed for a labor movement that thinks socially and acts politically—in the interests of its own class, not that of the bosses. This becomes more necessary than ever in the face of increasing imperialist war moves.

The tactical divisions in the ruling class are real, and we haven't found it difficult to explain the reasons for them. They enable us to see the dangerous character of the con being promoted by the bourgeois press—namely, that the debate in Congress pushes us further away from war. The truth is the opposite. The imperialist assumptions and goals shared by both Democratic and Republican party politicians and the bipartisan policies they have already set in motion—these are the very ingredients propelling forward the probability that the siege war will become a massive ground war (perhaps with a devastating air war as a prelude).

Workers and farmers, as well as any authentic opponent of Washington's course toward war, have no voice, no representatives in Congress of any kind. There have been tactical divisions and squabbles among bourgeois politicians in Congress, and between Congress and the White House, prior to every imperialist war in this century. There has also been a growing concentration of governmental power in the executive branch. But without exception, whenever the president has asked Congress for support in a war—whether in the form of a declaration of war such as in 1917 and 1941, or the Gulf of Tonkin resolution in 1964, or simply military funding—there has been overwhelming bipartisan support. This time around will be no different.

What the working-class movement needs is space to organize a broad public discussion of the connection between the rulers' war policies at home and abroad—a discussion with all those willing to debate the issues in a civil manner; space to organize active opposition to those policies in the factories, through our unions; space to take our protest to the streets; space to engage in politics in the class interests of workers, farmers, and our allies here and around the world. This debate should be organized above all among the almost half-million citizen-soldiers sent to the Arabian desert by Frank Lorenzo's friends in Washington.

Those who are going to have to fight and die in any war waged by the bipartisan rulers of this country should have the direct say over whether or not such a war is declared. On the face of it, that simply seems decent and just. But there's a lot more to it than that. For the question of war poses the biggest single problem facing the working class: we have no independent political organization, no political voice of our own, no policies that advance our class interests against those who are responsible for exploitation, oppression, and war.

The working class has no foreign policy. The labor movement has no foreign policy. The labor *officialdom* faithfully pushes the foreign policy of the employers and does what the bosses tell them to do. But the labor *movement*—the workers, the ranks, who are the unions—has no foreign policy. The classes who die in the wars waged by the bosses' parties and government—and who are pitted in those wars against working people like ourselves in other countries—have no foreign policy.

Many workers agree that it's unacceptable for the bosses to have a monopoly over setting all sorts of other policies: the policies that govern our unions; health and safety policies and conditions in the mines and factories; work rules on the job; the right to slash our wages or throw us out of work; the right to bust our unions and keep up production with scab labor.

But when it comes to foreign policy, the monopoly by the bosses is still largely accepted as almost a fact of life. The spectrum of valid choices is set by their two political parties. What's more, their foreign policy is viewed as "ours," the foreign policy of "our" country. But countries don't have policies. Countries are divided into social classes, and classes have foreign policies. And the foreign policy of the capitalist class in this country—and in every other capitalist country, everywhere in the world—is not "ours," it's "theirs." As Malcolm X taught us, working people in this country are not "Americans," we're the *victims* of this kind of Americanism.

Workers have no military policy, either. The labor movement has no military policy. Only the ruling class has a military policy. It begins with the hired thugs and the cops they use to bust up our strikes, to ride in scab trucks in West Virginia or in Bayside, Queens. And it goes right on through the organization of massive imperialist armed forces.

But the working class needs our own military policy as well as our own foreign policy. And there are layers of workers in recent years who have learned why, even if they haven't yet drawn this conclusion or thought of it this way. The *Daily News* strikers who have been victims of the goon squads brought in by management are learning about the military policy of the bosses; so are the coal miners, paperworkers, meat-packers, and others whose picket lines have been attacked by cops, whether "private" or "public." Also learning about it today are the workers and farmers in uniform—the cannon fodder (a term that has horrible concrete meaning in face of today's march toward a desert war of heavily armored armies) who make up the armed forces used by the imperialists to fight *their* wars to advance *their* class interests.

As long as capitalism and imperialism exist, there will be no peace. As long as the working class has no political party of our own—no labor party based on the unions and independent of the imperialist Democratic and Republican parties—we will have no effective mass political organization to resist the war policies of the employing class by counterposing and fighting for our own foreign policy and military policy. And we will have no political party of our own to organize a fight against the bosses' war on our rights, our living standards, and our unions here at home, either. Instead, we will always be facing the framework of political choices set by *their* parties.

Let the people vote on war

For the same reasons, communists are raising as part of our working-class campaign against the imperialist war that the people in this country should have the right to vote on war.

The point here is not to divert the energies of workers, farmers, and other opponents of the war into electoral channels—there will be plenty of referenda to do that. The point is just the opposite. Our demand is that the question of war and peace be taken out of the hands of the Democratic and Republican politicians, out of the hands of Congress and the White House, and be taken into the factories and into the streets.

We know that the imperialists always seek to tighten

and restrict the space to organize and practice politics when they go to war. That's what happened during the first and second world wars, during the Korean War, and during the Vietnam War. And it will happen again. Many of us remember the so-called Cointelpro spying, disruption, and harassment operations organized by the FBI, CIA, local police "red squads," and other government cop agencies during the period of the Vietnam War. The Socialist Workers Party was a direct victim of those assaults, along with others involved in the fight against the war, in the struggle for Black liberation, and in other social and political struggles. Recognizing this reality puts a special premium on vanguard workers treasuring and fighting for every inch of space we can.

That's why thinking workers pay special attention to any group of individuals and organizations who want to reach out and use democratic rights to publicly oppose the war drive—to discuss, to debate, to march; to initiate public protests, rallies, teach-ins, demonstrations. Those activities help create greater space for discussion and action around the war, greater space for the working class to get involved in politics.

This is the opposite of the terrain to which the capitalist rulers always seek to restrict the discussions and decisions on war. We are told that a great debate is taking place on Capitol Hill today on launching the war against Iraq. But it's a debate that involves at tops 535 people— 536 if you include the vice president—most of them millionaires, and all of them (Democrats, Republicans, and their "socialist" subspecies alike) opponents of independent political action by the working-class movement. These are the same people who have led workers and farmers into every bloody war in this century.

The fight against the war and the fight to defend democratic rights necessitates the broadest forum for public debate and exchange of views, as well. The bourgeois politicians will try to block such discussion. And as in the past, the union bureaucrats, petty-bourgeois pacifists, Stalinists, and social democrats will often join them in this reactionary effort—usually in the name of supporting this or that proposal or election campaign by a capitalist politician.

The working class, on the other hand, has every interest in promoting such discussion. Political clarity becomes more important than ever, and such clarity can be advanced only through *political differentiation.* That's why we advocate the norms of civil discussion—the right to express your point of view, to argue for it without fear of verbal abuse or physical recriminations—inside the workers' movement. This also means having the courage to clarify differences—which often reflect conflicting class outlooks and interests—rather than paper them over.

At the same time, proponents of a wide range of different views can and will join together to act, to organize, and to participate in antiwar demonstrations and other public protest actions. Communist workers are the most energetic advocates of such united action for common goals, and the staunchest opponents of efforts to exclude individuals or organizations from such efforts because of their political views.

We seek to draw more workers, more soldiers, more farmers into these activities, so that those who have been struggling against the employers' offensive in this country can become part of the debate and a growing component of the fight against the war drive.

22 months on the picket line
A chronicle

1976

After claiming it was bankrupt in 1975, Eastern Airlines wins the first of several rounds of concessions extracted from Machinists, flight attendants, and pilots. Frank Borman is Eastern's president.

1983

Eastern unions agree to accept a further round of deep-going pay cuts: Machinists and flight attendants take 18 percent cut, pilots 22 percent. A pay cut of 18 percent is forced on noncontract workers. Together unions and noncontract workers give up $360 million.

Frank Lorenzo spearheads a union-busting drive at Continental Airlines, owned by Texas Air Corporation.

1986

Borman demands and gets another 20 percent pay cut from pilots and flight attendants. The International Association of Machinists refuses cuts, despite Borman's threat to sell the airline. Eastern is sold to Frank Lorenzo's Texas Air.

1987

October 19—Contract talks start between Eastern and the IAM. The company demands $150 million in concessions from the Machinists. Some 7,000 union and nonunion workers are permanently laid off over the next sixteen months.

December—The IAM's contract expires. Workers remain on the job while negotiations continue.

1988

January 26—The National Mediation Board steps in at the request of both parties.

September—The Machinists vote 7,596 to 90 to reject Eastern's concession-contract demands.

1989

February 2—The National Mediation Board announces that talks are at an impasse. A thirty-day "cooling-off" period begins.

February 7—Seventeen hundred IAM members at Eastern's Miami maintenance base walk off the job to protest disciplinary measures taken against three workers. Hundreds are subsequently suspended for periods of ten to thirty days.

February 15—The union reports that IAM members at Eastern have voted by a 97 percent majority to strike when the cooling-off period ends at midnight March 3. Seventy-seven percent of the 8,500 eligible members voted.

February 21—The AFL-CIO officialdom urges President George Bush to appoint an emergency board to head off a strike for at least sixty days.

February 24—The National Mediation Board also recommends Bush appoint an emergency board—a call that is subsequently rejected. The Transport Workers Union (TWU) announces that the flight attendants' executive board has voted unanimously to back a strike by the Machinists.

March 1—Lorenzo offers pilots a five-year contract, seeking $64 million in wage and benefit concessions.

March 3—The Air Line Pilots Association (ALPA) votes to back a Machinists' strike. All IAM members are locked out by Lorenzo.

March 4, 12:01 a.m.—The 8,500 IAM members—ramp service workers, mechanics, aircraft cleaners, stock clerks, and facility cleaners—strike Eastern Airlines. Honoring the picket line are 5,900 flight attendants and 3,400 pilots. Eastern's operations come to a virtual standstill.

March 5—Injunctions are issued to prevent Machinists from setting up secondary picket lines at commuter railroads in New York, northern New Jersey, Philadelphia, and elsewhere, which had been set to go up March 6. The IAM states it will abide by the injunctions.

March 6-7—Eastern lays off 9,500 reservation clerks, ticket agents, office workers, and other noncontract employees.

March 9—Eastern files for bankruptcy in the federal bankruptcy court in New York. Proceedings are to be overseen by Judge Burton Lifland.

March 10—The bankruptcy court grants Eastern permission to pay management and scabs. Eastern begins offering $12 fares on its Northeast shuttle to drum up business.

March 10-19—Unionists mobilize at airports around the country to back strikers. The passenger load on Eastern's shuttle begins to drop after several days. Eastern starts hiring scab pilots.

March 22-24—Judge Lifland orders strike pickets not to "harass" passengers at New York's La Guardia Airport and Boston's Logan Airport. He also denies the unions' request that Eastern pay strikers wages owed them for their last week of work.

April—Across the United States, strikers begin picketing Eastern's scab-hiring sessions for flight attendants and mechanics.

April 5—After working without a contract for over fourteen months, 1,700 coal miners belonging to the United

Mine Workers of America (UMWA) walk off the job at the Pittston Coal Group's mines in Virginia and West Virginia. Later, two hundred Pittston miners in Kentucky will also join the strike.

April 6—A group of investors headed by Peter Ueberroth proposes to buy Eastern for $464 million. Union officials agree to $210 million in concessions and five-year contracts if the sale goes through.

A rally in support of the strike draws 300 in San Juan, Puerto Rico.

April 9—Contingents of Eastern strikers from Miami, New York, and other cities march in a massive abortion rights demonstration in Washington, D.C.

April 11—The sale to Ueberroth collapses at midnight after Lorenzo refuses to agree to a court-appointed trustee to run the airline until the sale is finalized.

April 24—Eastern president Phillip Bakes announces a plan to break the strike by "reorganizing" the airline as a smaller, nonunion carrier, selling off $1.8 billion in assets.

April 30—Ten thousand people attend a rally in Castlewood, Virginia, to support the striking Pittston miners. Attendance is swelled by outrage over police violence against peaceful picketers at Pittston earlier in the week.

May 13—Chicago commodities speculator Joseph Ritchie submits a bid to buy Eastern.

May 24—The bankruptcy court approves the sale of Eastern's shuttle to Donald Trump.

May 30—Striking Eastern and Pittston workers begin a joint twelve-day tour of West Virginia, Virginia, southwestern Pennsylvania, and eastern Kentucky to build solidarity for the two strikes.

June 2—Union officials announce their willingness to give up to $400 million in one year in concessions to make the Ritchie buyout possible. The AFL-CIO officialdom offers an additional $50 million.

June 5—The bankruptcy court concludes that the Ritchie

bid is not viable.

June 7—Trump takes over the northeast shuttle. Union officials agree to return to work there, and picket lines come down. Flight attendants and pilots are to work under an extension of the old Eastern contract; the Machinists report for work without any contract. The shuttle starts operations the following day.

June 11—Hundreds of Eastern strikers attend a Charleston, West Virginia, rally of 12,000 in support of the Pittston miners. The action is the biggest labor demonstration in West Virginia in fifteen years.

June 12—Walkouts by UMWA miners begin in southern West Virginia in solidarity with the Pittston strike. Over the next six weeks, these spread rapidly throughout the coal fields, involving 44,000 miners in eleven states.

June 29—Machinists at the Trump Shuttle vote by a substantial margin to accept a six-month union-weakening contract.

July 2—Rallies and expanded picket lines are held in many cities to protest Eastern's increase of daily flights from 80 to 226. Eastern slashes fares to lure passengers.

July 8—A scab baggage handler is killed at the Atlanta airport in an on-the-job accident.

July 14—Eastern announces losses of $81.6 million in April, $82.4 million in May, and $61.8 million in June.

Hundreds of strikers and strike supporters march to New York's La Guardia Airport, blocking the roadway and entrances to Eastern's departure areas for several hours.

July 20—Pittston begins negotiations with the miners' union. Shortly afterward, the last UMWA members striking in solidarity with the Pittston miners return to work.

July 28–August 4—Rallies and marches are held to protest Eastern's increase of flights to 350 a day.

Early August—At the urging of top ALPA officers, more than 200 pilots cross the picket line, along with hundreds of flight attendants. Eastern pilots vote to continue backing the strike.

August 15—Eastern flights increase to 390 a day.

August 21—Machinists at New York's La Guardia Airport and other unionists hold the first of several informational picket lines at Hudson General, one of several IAM-organized subcontracting companies hired to do ramp and other work for Eastern.

August 24—Texas Air announces it may sell some or all of Continental. A few days later, Eastern reveals it may fall $400 million short of the cash projected in its reorganization plan.

September 4—Eastern strikers lead Labor Day demonstrations in New York and other cities.

September 6—Some 1,000 strikers and strike supporters rally at the Capitol in Washington, D.C., to mark the last stop of a 3,000-mile "Journey for Justice" strike caravan.

September 7—Eastern's daily flights increase to 600. Strikers hold protests in many cities.

September 12—The bankruptcy court approves the sale of nine of Eastern's thirteen gates in Philadelphia, along with other assets, to Midway Airlines, a largely non-union carrier.

September 17—Ninety-eight striking Pittston miners begin a three-day occupation of Pittston's Moss No. 3 plant in Carbo, Virginia, the second-largest coal-processing plant in the country. Outside, thousands of miners and supporters, including Eastern strikers, rally in support.

October—A majority of IAM-organized fuelers at Ogden Allied at Washington, D.C.'s National Airport sign a petition urging IAM International officials to allow them not to fuel Eastern planes. Eastern increases daily flights to 700; the IAM reports that the flight schedule is being met by using twenty-eight Continental planes and crews.

Late October–early November—Rallies, human billboards, and airport walk-throughs take place in many cities. A human billboard of 1,500 is held in Miami on October 23. On October 29, 100 striking coal miners join a walk-through at the Greater Pittsburgh International Airport.

November 1—Unionists in Cincinnati picket the start-up of three Continental flights there. In Boston, strike supporters appeal to students not to fly Eastern or Continental over the holidays.

November 10—The bankruptcy court enters an injunction against the IAM aimed at restricting picketing and other strike activity at airports and other sites.

November 19—A statewide strike support march in Miami draws 1,000. Pittston miners come down to join strikers at "Miami Camp Solidarity."

November 21—President Bush vetoes legislation to establish a "blue-ribbon" panel to investigate the Eastern conflict and recommend solutions to it.

November 22—ALPA's Master Executive Council ends the pilots' sympathy strike at Eastern. The TWU leadership does the same for the flight attendants the following day. Lorenzo says there are no jobs for pilots or flight attendants. The IAM leadership declares the Machinists' strike solid.

November 27-28—The Nordic Transport Workers Federation—representing transport workers' unions in Sweden, Norway, and Denmark—issues a strong statement in support of the Eastern strike.

December 9—A federal grand jury in Brooklyn states it is weighing whether to file criminal charges against Eastern for safety violations at New York's Kennedy International Airport.

December 19—American Airlines announces it is buying Eastern's Latin American routes and other assets for $471 million. The IAM reports that Eastern's passenger load is 48 percent of capacity.

December 22—Eastern makes known a reduction in daily flights from 830 to 803.

December 28—Layoffs of 600 Eastern scab employees are announced, along with wage cuts for half the remaining scab work force.

1990

January 1—A tentative contract is announced in the Pittston strike. The agreement comes after Secretary of Labor Elizabeth Dole had appointed a special mediator. Terms of the agreement are not made public.

January 11—The federal grand jury investigation of safety violations widens to include La Guardia Airport.

January 15—Strikers in Atlanta, Miami, New York, and other cities join activities commemorating the birthday of Martin Luther King, Jr.

January 19—An eight-month boycott of Eastern led by the Bermuda Industrial Union forces Eastern to cancel its daily flight in and out of Bermuda. Eastern soon cancels flights to nine other Caribbean destinations.

January 22-24—An IAM legislative conference in Washington, D.C., maps an effort to get Congress to override Bush's veto of a blue-ribbon panel.

January 24—Texas Air stock drops by 16 percent in one day, closing at $7.37. It continues to sink in following days, down from a 1989 high of $24.

January 25—Lorenzo presents another reorganization plan to Eastern's unsecured creditors' committee. He proposes that of the $1 billion the creditors are owed they will get 10 percent when Eastern emerges from bankruptcy, 70 percent over the next ten years without interest, and the remaining 20 percent in company stock.

January 30—A committee representing Eastern's preferred stockholders tells the federal bankruptcy court it has lost faith in Eastern's management. It calls for drastic steps to salvage the airline's remaining value.

February 3—Machinists at La Guardia Airport in New York hold the first of regular biweekly expanded solidarity picket lines, following the example of strikers in Los Angeles.

February 6—Eastern admits 1989 losses of $852.3 million—a record for the airline industry. Texas Air as a whole lost $885.6 million.

February 19—Striking Pittston miners vote to accept a new contract and end their walkout, which has lasted almost eleven months. Many vow to continue solidarity with the Eastern strikers.

February 22—Lorenzo reaches agreement with unsecured creditors. The creditors are promised $300 million in cash and $190 million in eight-year notes.

March 2—Over 9,000 members of the Amalgamated Transit Union at Greyhound go on strike after refusing to accept a contract that included no wage hike, cuts in benefits, and union-weakening provisions.

March 3-4—Backed by the AFL-CIO, strikers and strike supporters from many unions hold rallies, mass pickets, airport walk-throughs, benefits, and other activities to mark the one-year anniversary of the Eastern strike. Ten thousand people participate in at least twenty-seven cities in the United States, Canada, and Puerto Rico.

March 7—Congress votes not to override Bush's veto of a blue-ribbon panel. The House vote to override is 261 to 160, short of the necessary two-thirds majority.

March 22—ALPA reports an interim agreement with Eastern for pilots who crossed the picket line. Wages will be slashed 25 percent and retirement benefits cut.

March 27—Eastern announces it is unable to meet the terms of its February agreement with the airline's creditors. Lorenzo subsequently offers 5 cents on the dollar in immediate cash and 20 cents on the dollar in secured notes.

March 29—It is announced that in voting earlier in the month the Aircraft Mechanics Fraternal Association (AMFA)—a company-minded outfit that seeks to raid the IAM of its mechanics—has defeated the IAM, 68 to

18, in a union representation vote among mechanics at the Trump Shuttle.

April 3—Eastern's unsecured creditors unanimously reject Lorenzo's latest offer.

April 9—Eastern's preferred shareholders give Lorenzo a vote of no confidence by filing their own reorganization plan.

April 10—Eastern's unsecured creditors ask the bankruptcy court to appoint a trustee to run the airline.

April 18—Declaring Texas Air "not competent" to complete the reorganization of Eastern, the bankruptcy court removes Lorenzo from management of Eastern Airlines and appoints Martin Shugrue as trustee.

April 25—Five hundred Eastern strikers and supporters hold a "Farewell to Lorenzo" action on the Miami picket line. Police attack the picketers, hospitalizing a seventy-year-old retired unionist and arresting one striker. The cop violence is widely seen on local television.

May 3—Hundreds of unionists hold a rally in New York outside the Greyhound terminal. The action is billed as an act of solidarity with strikers at Eastern and Greyhound and garment workers on strike at Domsey Trading Company in Brooklyn. That same day 1,500 delegates at the Pennsylvania AFL-CIO state convention hold a solidarity rally in Pittsburgh.

May 12—More than 150 unionists and farmers rally in Marshalltown, Iowa, to back the Eastern and Greyhound strikes. The rally is sponsored by the Central Iowa Labor Alliance.

June 17—Eastern trustee Shugrue launches a "100 days" campaign, saying, "For the next 100 days Eastern is going to get a little better every day." A massive television and newspaper advertising campaign begins.

June 20—Eastern issues a memo to employees reporting that meetings have been held with two major airlines about "future business relationships." The same day striking Machinists and members of ALPA in Atlanta start visiting hundreds of travel agents to counter Shugrue's "100 days" campaign.

Nelson Mandela arrives in New York City, where he will begin an eight-city U.S. tour. He is greeted by a crowd of 750,000, including a contingent of Eastern strikers.

June 21—It is reported that Shugrue will ask unsecured creditors and the bankruptcy court to approve a $50 million withdrawal from Eastern's escrow accounts to make lease payments on the airline's planes. An earlier withdrawal of $80 million was approved in April; Shugrue now says the first withdrawal was earmarked to cover operating expenses only through June.

June 28—An Eastern Boeing 727 returns to Tampa, Florida, when an ice-clogged fuel line shuts down one of its engines after takeoff. This follows on the heels of another incident in early June when an Eastern DC-9 made an emergency landing in Atlanta after one of its two engines was damaged by a blown tire on takeoff.

June 30—More than six hundred Machinists and their supporters march around the Miami International Airport to demand, "Contract now!" Other protests take place in Detroit and Boston.

July 1—Two hundred Machinists, coal miners, steelworkers, Greyhound workers, and members of a dozen other unions hold a rally and walk-through at the Greater Pittsburgh International Airport to support the Eastern strike.

July 3—*USA Today* releases a survey reporting that 59 percent of travel agents questioned gave Eastern D's or F's on how well the airline serves business travelers. Seventy percent picked Eastern as the airline business travelers most often refuse to fly.

July 5—An Eastern DC-9 flying from Newark to Atlanta makes an emergency landing in Philadelphia after the plane's nose blew off in mid-air, leaving wires dangling and the windshield broken. One passenger reports the plane did several free falls prior to landing.

July 13—Shugrue holds a press conference in New York following a meeting with unsecured creditors. He admits Eastern continues to lose $1 million a day and will lose hundreds of millions by the end of the year. Shugrue also confirms that Eastern is carrying out "substantive" discussions with Northwest on a possible buyout deal.

July 17—An IAM District 100 bulletin includes a report from the July issue of the *IMF News,* the International Metalworkers Federation newspaper, stating that the union federation has called on its 13 million members around the world not to fly Eastern.

July 25—U.S. Attorney Andrew Maloney announces at a press conference that Eastern and ten of its management employees have been charged in a sixty-count indictment for safety violations, obstruction of justice, conspiracy to defraud the government, and other crimes.

August 2—Iraq invades Kuwait. Within days the U.S. government and its allies begin amassing troops and war matériel in preparation for war. Eastern is one of the commercial airline companies that the Pentagon will use to ferry troops to the Arab-Persian Gulf.

August 4—Two hundred fifty Eastern strikers and other unionists form a human billboard across an overpass leading to La Guardia Airport. Other actions are held in Washington, D.C., and Boston. The previous day, a demonstration outside Miami's Eastern gate drew 125.

August 9—Lorenzo steps down as chief executive of Continental Airlines and announces he is selling most of his stake in Continental Airlines Holdings, Inc. (formerly Texas Air) to Scandinavian Airlines System (SAS). As a condition of the sale, he agrees to quit the airline industry for at least seven years.

August 14—Judge Lifland grants Eastern "emergency relief" from its obligation to abide by the pilots' contract and paves the way for the airline to cut pilots' wages by 20 percent.

September 3—Strikers and supporters lead off marches, speak at rallies, and organize speaking events at Labor Day activities across the United States. They use the opportunity to reach thousands of workers by selling buttons and T-shirts and distributing informational leaflets.

September 6—Eastern's attempt to start up flights out of Roanoke, Virginia, is met by a protest of over fifty unionists and supporters, outnumbering the few Eastern passengers.

September 12—Eastern quietly ends the "100 days" campaign. The September 12 IAM District 100 strike bulletin reports that the passenger load factor for the ninety-ninth day of the campaign was 42 percent, almost 40 percent below what the airline needs to break even. Eastern continues to lose more than $1 million a day.

September 15—Eastern misses a $95 million payment deadline to the Pension Benefit Guaranty Corporation. Later an agreement is reached between the pension agency and Continental Airlines Holdings Inc. making the latter liable for up to $680 million in payments owed by Eastern.

October—Several other airline companies indicate they are bidding to purchase parts of Eastern.

October 25—After demanding millions of dollars in concessions, New York's *Daily News* locks out 2,200 workers and forces them to strike. The *Daily News* produces the newspaper with scab labor, but working people refuse to buy it and discourage its sale from newsstands.

November 13—Eastern acknowledges third-quarter losses of $252 million, bringing the year's total losses thus far to $424.9 million.

November 27—The bankruptcy court gives Eastern $135 million out of the company's escrow accounts to keep the airline operating.

December 1—Federal agents raid Eastern's Miami headquarters and seize safety logs, as part of investigating continued violations by the airline.

December 3—Continental Airlines Holdings Inc. files for bankruptcy.

1991

January 18—Eastern Airlines management announces the carrier will shut down operations at midnight. Shugrue says the following day that the airline had "run out of time and resources." Strikers in Miami, New York, Atlanta, and other cities celebrate the airline's demise.

January 22—Officials of the International Association of Machinists announce the strike is over. "The future will be brighter for all workers because of your courage," writes IAM president George Kourpias to the strikers. Strikers take down their picket lines on January 24, the 692d day of the Machinists' strike against Eastern Airlines.

February 27—In a plea-bargaining agreement, Eastern admits it is guilty of falsifying maintenance records and other safety violations and is ordered to pay $3.5 million in fines. A week later, five additional Eastern managers from Atlanta's Hartsfield Airport are indicted on similar charges.

Lessons for today's fighters

Teamster Rebellion ($14.95), **Teamster Power** ($16.95),
Teamster Politics ($16.95), **Teamster Bureaucracy** ($17.95)
Farrell Dobbs

The 1985-86 Hormel Meat-Packers Strike in Austin, Minnesota
Fred Halstead, $2.50

Labor's Giant Step
Twenty Years of the CIO
Art Preis, $23.95

"Opening Guns of World War III: Washington's Assault on Iraq"
Jack Barnes
in *New International* 7, $10.00

COINTELPRO: The FBI's Secret War on Political Freedom
Nelson Blackstock, $14.95

The Frame-Up of Mark Curtis
A Packinghouse Worker's Fight for Justice
Margaret Jayko, $5.00

Out Now!
*A Participant's Account of the Movement in
the United States against the Vietnam War*
Fred Halstead, $29.95

Revolutionary Continuity
Birth of the Communist Movement: 1918-1922
Farrell Dobbs, $15.95

The Communist Manifesto
Karl Marx, Frederick Engels, $2.50

In Defense of Socialism
Fidel Castro, $12.95

Nelson Mandela: Speeches 1990
'Intensify the Struggle to Abolish Apartheid,' $5.00

The Revolution Betrayed
What Is the Soviet Union and Where Is It Going?
Leon Trotsky, $18.95

Cosmetics, Fashions, and the Exploitation of Women
Joseph Hansen, Evelyn Reed
Introduction by Mary-Alice Waters, $11.95

ORDER FROM PATHFINDER. SEE FRONT OF BOOK FOR ADDRESSES.

The Changing Face of U.S. Politics
The Proletarian Party and the Trade Unions
Jack Barnes

Building a party of socialist workers in a world of imperialist wars, economic crises, and assaults on the unions—a world where the battles by the rank and file play an increasingly central role. 346 pp., $18.95

Teamster Bureaucracy
Farrell Dobbs

How the class-struggle leaders of the 1930s Midwest Teamsters union organized to oppose World War II and the bosses' attacks at home. Written by a central leader of this fight jailed for his opposition to the war. 304 pp. $17.95

U.S. Hands Off the Mideast!
Cuba Speaks Out at the United Nations
Fidel Castro, Ricardo Alarcón
Introduction by Mary-Alice Waters

The case against Washington's war in the Mideast, as presented in the United Nations. Includes Security Council resolutions and a detailed chronology of events. 126 pp. $9.95

Trade Unions in the Epoch of Imperialist Decay
Leon Trotsky, Karl Marx

Two revolutionary working-class leaders discuss the tasks of unions and their relationship to workers' fight for economic justice and political power. 156 pp. $13.95

Malcolm X Talks to Young People

Malcolm X denounces U.S.-organized wars against national liberation struggles in Vietnam and Africa and describes the challenges young people face in the fight for a just world. A new collection. 110 pp. $9.95